Holistic Ministry
and
Cross-cultural Mission
in
Luke-Acts

By
Glenn Rogers

Published by

Mission And Ministry Resources

Visit Our Website At:

www.missionandministryresources.net

TABLE OF CONTENTS

4

Introduction

Luke's two-volume work comprises over twenty-five percent of the material found in the New Testament. Yet despite his prominence we know little about the man. Luke was a second generation believer, not Jewish, a doctor, and was, at least some of the time, a traveling companion of Paul—engaged with the apostle in holistic, cross-cultural ministry and mission in the Hellenistic world (Geldenhuys 1951:15-22). What does Luke's record of holistic, cross-cultural ministry and mission in the first century suggest to us as a community of faith today? The purpose of this study is to: 1) examine the holistic nature of ministry in the context of cross-cultural mission as it is described in Luke-Acts, and 2) discuss the implications of those factors for the church today.

There are several assumptions that need to be clarified before proceeding. Since this study does not involve a detailed analysis of the complete text of Luke-Acts, it is not necessary to include a thorough discussion of background considerations such as authorship, date, sources, purpose, audience, and so forth. Modern scholars have discussed those issues at length for well over one hundred years and duplicating them here would serve no useful purpose. Norval Geldenhuys has an excellent discussion of background issues related to Luke-Acts, as does Joseph

Fitzmyer, F. F. Bruce, I. Howard Marshall, and Timothy Luke Johnson.

One foundational assumption in this work is that Paul's occasional traveling companion and fellow laborer in the kingdom, identified as Luke, is the author of Luke-Acts and probably wrote his two-volume work in the mid to late first century, sometime between 60 and 85 AD.

Another assumption is that Luke was doing a good deal more than merely recording history. Hans Conzelmann observes that "one of the main insights of Form Criticism was that the Gospels are in their nature and purpose not a historical record or a biography of Jesus; their purpose is the proclamation of saving events, though, it is true, of such as in the author's view have taken place in history" (1961:10). One of the foundational assumptions of this study is the historicity of Luke's information. However, detailing history for the sake of history is not Luke's purpose. While the historical framework in which the events he details took place is important for Luke, his *multi-layered* purpose is far more theological than historical.

One of Luke's many theological goals was to demonstrate that the community of faith (which had become largely non-Jewish in ethnic makeup by the time he wrote his books) traced its roots to the Jewish people and the promises God had made to them centuries before. As his story unfolds, it is clear that while the roots of Christianity are Jewish, the branches are multicultural.

Luke's intention was that Luke-Acts be read and studied together so that the progression of events as they occurred could be linked to the historical contexts in which they took place, thus lending credibility to the account. Luke informs his readers of his purpose or goal in his prolog, Lk. 1:1-4. He describes his work as a *narrative* which he intends to write in order, or sequence (Johnson 2000:Vol. 4, 405). His reason for doing this is so Theophilus, to whom Luke addresses both his books, will have complete confidence in the things he has been taught regarding faith in Jesus. Whether Theophilus was a new believer being instructed and strengthened by Luke, or whether he had only recently heard the gospel and was contemplating a faith response and needed additional teaching and reassurance before making a commitment is open to discussion (Larkin 1998:152-155). Either way, Luke's goal is to place the events he records in his two books in a historical framework with which Theophilus and other readers will be familiar—the sociopolitical environment of the first century Roman world. Though Luke's purpose is more theological than historical, it is fair to say that he is concerned about history. His work is theological/historical in nature.

To accomplish this duel theological/historical purpose, Luke selected a narrative methodology. Luke expects his readers to be impacted by the story as it unfolds before them (Johnson 2000:Vol. 4, 405). His ultimate goals can only be realized as he is allowed to speak through the complete narrative of both his books. The Gospel and Acts taken together represent the story Luke intended to tell. Only when they are read, interpreted and applied together can Luke's intention for his work be realized.

What then, was Luke's intention or purpose for writing? Marshall suggests that it is "fairly certain" that Luke wrote for an "urban church community in the Hellenistic world" (1978:33). Fitzmyer suggests that Luke wanted to convey to a non-Jewish church community that the faith they had embraced had its roots in Jewish history. Further, he wanted them to understand that what God did in the life and ministry of Jesus and in the early days of the community of Jewish believers was according to God's promises (1970:9). God had fulfilled his promises to Israel, and he will keep his promises to all who trust him (Johnson 2000:Vol.4, 407-408). Israel was given the first opportunity to hear and respond to the message of mercy, grace and forgiveness through faith in Jesus. Many Israelites believed.

Unfortunately, many of them did not. God then made the same mercy, grace and forgiveness available to all people, which, as it turns out, was his plan all along. One of Luke's goals is to demonstrate over the course of his two-volume narrative how the story began in the *particular* context of Judaism and spread to the *universal* context of all people (Dollar 1990:264-266).

Another of Luke's goals, revealed as his narrative unfolds, is the inclusive nature of the community of faith. Not only are the respectable of society welcome to respond to God's offer of grace and mercy, so are the marginalized— the poor, the oppressed, the sick, women, children, tax collectors and sinners (Harms 1999:70-75).

The inclusion of socially unacceptable people, along with non-Jewish people—regardless of their social standing—into the community of faith required the crossing of social and cultural boundaries, the ultimate of which involved table fellowship. To sit down with a person (or recline at table) and eat together implied equality and acceptance. One of Luke's purposes in his two-volume work was to demonstrate that not only was God interested in the socially unacceptable within Israel, but also in those who had always be considered culturally unacceptable—non-Jewish people. That such was God's intention, and that a faithful community of believers could and would transverse those social and cultural boundaries is demonstrated in Luke's historical/theological narrative (Sweetland 1990:126-140).

Related to the inclusive spirit of the community of faith in Jesus is the holistic nature of their outreach. Those who were previously excluded will now be included. They may be hungry. They may be harassed and tormented by demons. They may be destitute. They may be sick. Perhaps they are orphaned or widowed. Perhaps they are old. Regardless of their condition, to be included in the community of faith requires that the community minister to their needs—whatever those needs may be. Only the kind of holistic approach to ministry that Luke reveals in the course of his two-volume narrative will accomplish God's purpose for loving and saving all people (Maynard-Reid 1997).

Another of Luke's narrative goals was to demonstrate the role of the Holy Spirit in the life and ministry of Jesus and in the community of faith. Luke does not attempt to accomplish this by declaring a formal or systematic pneumatology. Rather, over the course of his narrative, Luke reveals a Holy Spirit who is active in inspiring and empowering Jesus and his followers (Shelton 1991). It is the Spirit who directs ministry and mission and empowers people—even Jesus—to accomplish God's work. The same Spirit who guided and empowered Jesus guides and empowers his followers. They, therefore, are fully prepared for ministry and mission.

Yet another of Luke's goals in writing is his concern to communicate what it means to be a disciple of Jesus. What does it mean to be a member of a Spirit guided, Spirit empowered community of faith, practicing holistic evangelism and ministry among all people, including the marginalized of society? Throughout his narrative, Luke demonstrates what it means to be a disciple in such a community of people. His story illustrates several important features of discipleship including: 1) one's attitude towards oneself, expressed in an attitude of submissive servanthood, 2) one's attitude toward others, expressed in a willingness to love one's neighbors as much as oneself—even if those neighbors are the socially or culturally untouchable, and 3) one's attitude toward wealth and the material world in general, expressed in a willingness to reprioritize and sacrifice, putting spiritual things ahead of material things.

Undoubtedly, one could find additional "goals" in Luke's narrative, but these are sufficient to illustrate the point: Luke's purpose for writing is fully revealed as one reads and studies both his books, allowing him to demonstrate his intentions in recording specific the events in the ministry and mission of Jesus and his followers.

To this point, I have described and discussed Luke's work as *history* with a decided *theological* purpose or focus. This is an accurate description, but not as thorough as it might be. In addition to its historical/theological perspective, Luke's work must also be understood from a *missiological* perspective. Missiology is the study of mission—God's mission in the world (the *missio Dei*), and the church's participation with him in that mission. The themes that emerge in Luke's two-volume work make it distinctively missiological in focus and application. This is not to say that Luke consciously wrote from a missiological perspective. The development of missiology as an academic discipline is relatively new, originating in the mid-eighteen hundreds (Neely 2000:633-635). Obviously, Luke did not intend to address specific areas of missiological concern as a missiologist. As it happens, however, the areas of concern which interest missiologists are significant considerations in Luke's narrative. So whether he meant to or not, Luke produced a document which has significant missiological implications for the church today. The implications of the missiological themes present in Luke's writing are the focus of this study.

Chapter 1 focuses on the theological/missiological progression of Luke's narrative as it moves from a particular Palestinian Jewish context to a worldwide universal context including peoples of all ethnic groups. Luke's story begins with a Levite named Zechariah serving his priestly duty rotation at the temple in Jerusalem and ends with Paul in prison in Rome. A lot of theological/missiological ground is covered as the story unfolds, moving not only across time, but also across social and cultural boundaries as a community of Jewish believers is formed and eventually expands to include non-Jewish believers as well. The theological ground that is broken and the missiological precedents that are set in Luke's narrative challenge the church today to reexamine existing theological/missiological assumptions.

Chapter 2 focuses on Luke's presentation of the Holy Spirit. What was the Spirit's role related to witness about Jesus? What was the Spirit's role in the life and ministry of Jesus? What was his role in the life and ministry of Jesus' followers? Though Luke does not present a formal pneumatology, his focus on the Spirit's role in mission and ministry becomes a crucial factor for consideration today. Does the church today seek the Spirit's guidance in mission and ministry? To what extent? If the same Spirit that lived in and worked through Jesus and his early followers still lives in and works through believers today, can we expect the same kind of leadership and empowerment today the church experienced centuries ago? The theological/missiological implications of the Spirit's role in mission and ministry are staggering. If we deny the Spirit his rightful place in mission and ministry the consequences will be staggering. Likewise, if we give the Spirit his rightful place in mission and ministry the results will be completely different but just as staggering.

Chapter 3 focuses on the issue of table fellowship in Luke's story. Luke's narrative progresses from the socially acceptable Jewish priest, Zechariah, to his fiery son, John, who lives an isolated life, to a young rabbi named Jesus who associates with the socially unacceptable (tax collectors and sinners of all sorts). As Jews who become followers of Jesus preach to Samaritans, and ultimately to the non-Jewish people of the Hellenistic world, the issue of table fellowship, that is, of Jewish people eating with non-Jewish people—a practice that had always been forbidden—becomes a crucial issue. Has that which has always been unacceptable now become acceptable? What has changed? Why has it changed? How does the church of the first century cope with the change? What are the implications for the church today?

Chapter 4 focuses on the nature of discipleship in Luke's narrative. When Jesus invited people to follow him, what did he expect of them? What kinds of things do disciples do in Luke's story? What kinds of lives do they live? One of Luke's purposes for writing is to demonstrate the distinctive, holistic nature of Christian discipleship. But in Luke's narrative, that distinctive, holistic discipleship can be lived out in different cultural settings. Christian discipleship is not a cookie-cutter kind of conformity to a specific cultural form. It is a process of living out one's faith in a way that is consistent with God's expectations for individuals in the cultural context in which he or she lives— especially in light of the outward mission orientation that characterizes Jesus' followers. What are the implications of this for God's people? How does the community of faith nurture a sound, biblical faith in new believers and at the same time allow that faith to be contextualized and expressed in ways that are culturally appropriate for those new believers?

Chapter 5 focuses on the spiritual and social dynamics of holistic evangelism in Luke-Acts. Who did Jesus spend time with in his ministry? What did his ministry among those people include? In Luke's narrative, the marginalized of society—the poor, the sick, women, children, Samaritans, and other outcasts or untouchables— were the focus of ministry. In the Gospel, the *outcasts* are the marginalized of Jewish society and Samaritans. In Acts, the *outcasts* are Gentiles. In each context, these marginalized people experience holistic ministry. Hungry people are fed. Sick people are healed. Rejected people are accepted. All are welcomed into a community of faith that provides opportunities to receive and to give. With the overwhelming social challenges that exist today, how can the church maintain a proper balance between the spiritual and the social dynamics of the holistic outreach?

Chapter 6 focuses on the missiological implications of Luke-Acts for the church today. Any one of the areas discussed in chapters 1 through 5 presents a challenge for the church today. How does the church today find ways to acknowledge, analyze and *respond* to all five of those challenges? James warned against the danger of looking at oneself in a mirror and then turning away, forgetting what was apparent, doing nothing to remedy the deficiencies (Jas. 1:22-25). The challenges God's people face today are too great for us to neglect a single biblical consideration regarding ministry and mission in the world today.

CHAPTER 1

FROM PARTICULARISM TO UNIVERSALISM: THE THEOLOGICAL, MISSIOLOGICAL PROGRESSION OF LUKE-ACTS

Luke's narrative begins in the particular context of Judaism—a context of temple and priesthood, of covenant and promise, of incense and altar, of sacrifice and prayer, of ceremony and ritual, of expectation and hope. It was a culture rooted in God's selection of Abraham, and of Israel as the people of God. But for many Israelites in those days, the joy of God's special favor was overshadowed by the grim reality of political subjugation, for they lived out their faith under the suspicious, watchful eye and oppressive thumb of the Roman Empire. They would be glad when God finally fulfilled his promise and sent his messiah, who would free them from their oppressors, reestablishing them as a world power reminiscent of their beloved Davidic and Solomonic empires. Such was their hope. Such was their understanding of the Scriptures.

The Particularistic Jewish Context
in which Christianity Began

Luke begins his story within the very particular and unique context of Jewish religion and ritual. Zechariah was fulfilling his priestly duties at the temple according to the long established levitical rotation (1 Chron. 24:5-19) when an angel appeared to him. The angel explained that Zechariah and his wife, Elizabeth, would have a son who would be a great prophet, like Elijah had been. The child was to be named John. His work would result in many changes in the lives of individuals and in the nation of Israel.

From Zechariah and Elizabeth, Luke pushes his narrative forward, to a young woman named Mary, engaged to be married. She, too, would have a son. Jesus would be his name. His birth would not be a result of her relations with her husband to be, but would be the result of a supernatural conception by the power of the Holy Spirit. The child would be God's son. He would be given the throne of David, and would establish an eternal kingdom.

As Luke's story proceeds, Mary visits Elizabeth and praises God for what he is about to do (or is in the process of doing) among his people. Reminiscent of Hannah's prayer in 1 Samuel 2:1-10 (Ash 1972:Vol. 1, 42), Mary focuses on God's concern for the poor and oppressed, and how her and Elizabeth's pregnancies and the prophecies regarding their sons signal the beginning of the fulfillment of God's promises to Israel.

When John is born, Zechariah is filled with the Holy Spirit and praises the Lord for fulfilling his promises. Even though Jesus is yet to be born, the Spirit, through Zechariah, praises God for having completed an amazing thing among his people. The promises to David have been fulfilled. The words of the prophets have come true. Israel is rescued. The people are delivered. Forgiveness is realized. They can now serve the Lord in holiness and righteousness. Praise God for what he has done among his people!

Luke then proceeds to the birth of Jesus. It is a scant narrative, brief and to the point. The details of the physical birth are not given as much attention as is the angelic visitation to the shepherds afterwards, who are told that the promised messiah has come. Glory to God! The shepherds believe the heavenly chorus and go into the village to visit their new king.

Luke's story began with Zechariah at the temple but moved quickly to Elizabeth, Mary and the births of their sons. Now Luke returns to the temple setting as Joseph and Mary visit Jerusalem to complete their obligations as new parents under the Law of Moses. On this occasion, Joseph and Mary perform their legal responsibilities, and Simeon and Anna glorify God for what he has done in Israel.

Luke's next story point comes twelve years later when Jesus, during a Passover visit to Jerusalem, remained in the city without his parent's knowledge to discuss theology with the teachers of the law—at the temple. Scholars have noted how much of Luke's narrative, in both the Gospel and Acts, occurs in or around the temple (Dollar 1990:25-27). Why did Luke do this? To establish the connection between Judaism and Christianity for his non-Jewish readers.

Skipping another eighteen years, Luke turns to the ministry of John the Baptist. John, the fiery prophet who resembled Elijah, spoke about the coming messiah and called Israel to repentance. As a result of John's preaching many people repented and were baptized. Jesus, too, came to be baptized—though not because he needed to repent, for he had committed no sin. After Jesus is baptized, the Holy Spirit descends on him and God speaks to him, acknowledging Jesus as his much loved son.

Then comes Luke's lengthy accounting of Jesus' ancestors, traced from Joseph all the way back to Adam, which may have seemed strange to Luke's non-Jewish readers. But regardless of their reaction to the lengthy genealogy, Luke has demonstrated his point: the Jewish roots of the religious movement which, by the time Luke wrote, was largely non-Jewish in composition.

Is it by accident or coincidence that Luke's narrative begins so deeply rooted in Jewish culture? I do not believe so. I believe it was Luke's design to begin his story in the most Jewish (*particularistic*) context he could describe (priests, incense, angelic visitations, sacrifice, prophesy, fulfillment, circumcision, preaching, repentance, baptism), in order to set up a contrast with how the story would proceed, and ultimately how it would end—in a very non-Jewish (*universalistic*) context. His movement from the Jewish context to a non-Jewish context occurs slowly over the course of his story. But even in these early chapters, where his goal was to demonstrate the Jewish origins of the Christian faith, Luke hints at the universal nature of what God was doing in the world.

Hints at God's Universal Design in Luke

Luke 2:32

Simeon's prophecy concerning Jesus is the first hint in Luke's narrative that God's plan is not limited to the Jewish people. Speaking of the impact of Jesus' life and ministry, Simeon says, *"He is a light to reveal God to the nations, and he is the glory of your people Israel!"* (Lk.2:32). Jesus would reveal God to the *nations*, that is, to the nations other than the nation of Israel, who already knew God. The contrast between the Gentiles and Israel is clear (Liefeld 1984:848-849), and the astute reader will notice that from the very beginning God's plan was universal in design. As will become apparent as Luke's story unfolds, the revelation and realization of the universal nature of God's plan was a matter of timing.

Luke 4:16-28

The next obvious hint of the universal nature of God's plan comes when Jesus visits his hometown synagogue in Nazareth. Jesus was handed the scroll that contained the prophecy of Isaiah. The text Jesus read, as reported by Luke, appears to be a compilation of Isaiah 61:1 and 58:6 (Culpepper 1995:105), in which Jesus highlights the focus of his mission and ministry. Though astonished that Jesus applied the text to himself, no one seemed terribly upset until Jesus implied that as the Spirit-anointed messiah sent by God, he would go to the Gentiles (Green 1997:206-218). Elijah and Elisha served as examples of how God had sent his prophets to Gentile people instead of Israelites. Jesus' comment enraged the people and they intended to kill him. Johannes Nissen notes that 4:18-21 is as important to Luke's Gospel as the Great Commission is to Matthew's (1999:50-51). I agree, but would extend the text to include the entire incident, including Jesus' comment regarding the Gentiles, for it provides a glimpse of God's broader focus for the extent of Jesus' ministry.

Luke 7:1-10

Another hint of the universal nature of God's plan is Jesus' willingness to heal the servant of the Roman officer. Jesus is fully prepared to go to the man's home. The thought itself is scandalous! A Jewish rabbi going to the home of a Gentile! As it turned out, Jesus did not go to the man's home. But he would have. The reason he did not was because the man had so much faith. Jesus' comment that he had not found so much faith among Jewish people is an amazing compliment to the Gentile officer and a stinging

21

indictment of the Jews. When one combines Jesus' willingness to go to the home of a Gentile, with his comparative compliment of the man's faith, this text is clearly another hint that the social and cultural scope of God's plan was much broader than the Jews realized.

Luke 8:26-39

Luke's next hint regarding the universal scope of God's plan involves Jesus traveling to the far side of the Sea of Galilee into Gentile territory (Bock 1994:771). The fact that there were pig herders there is evidence that the region was not predominantly Jewish in population. Yet Jesus went there. Why? Luke does not explain. His mere presence there, however, with his followers, is significant. He was teaching his disciples that his mission included non-Jewish people—a lesson, unfortunately, that did not sink in.

Luke 10:1-24

The universality of God's plan is apparent in Luke 10:1-24, where Jesus sends out seventy-two (or seventy) disciples to preach (Dollar 1990:34). Jesus tells his followers not to worry about dietary concerns—an amazing comment from Jesus given the legal and ceremonial concerns related to food. They are to eat whatever is set before them without asking questions. If Jesus' followers are going only to Jewish people, it is unlikely the issue regarding food would even be raised. Perhaps not all Jews were as careful as they should have been in their dietary habits. But Jesus' specific focus on the issue seems to suggest that the problem could have been one he expected to come up frequently, thereby suggesting the presence of and interaction with non-Jewish people.

Luke 14:15-24

Another clue is Jesus' story of a man who prepared a great feast. Many people had been invited. Customarily those invited would have been of the same social class as the person hosting the event. When everything was ready and the guests were informed that it was time to attend the event, they made excuses as to why they could not attend. The validity (or lack thereof) of the excuses is not the point of the story. The point is that when the invited guests could not (or would not) attend, the host sent his servants out to recruit new guests. The new guests, however, were not of the same social class as the original invited guests. The new guests were the marginalized of society: the poor, the crippled, the lame and the blind. The original guests in the story represent the Jews. That the new, replacement guests were the marginalized of Jewish society represents at least the crossing of social boundaries. Robert Stine, however, suggests that Luke's readers would have understood those marginalized people as representative of the Gentiles (1992:393), representing the crossing not only of social, but of cultural boundaries as well.

Luke 10:25-37 and 17:11-19

Other hints into the universal scope of God's mission may be Jesus' illustration of who acted neighborly—the Samaritan (Lk. 10:25-37), and the one leper who returned to thank Jesus for his healing—also a Samaritan (Lk. 17:11-19) (Harms 1999:70). While the Samaritans may not have been thought of as Gentiles (Dollar discusses questions related to the Jewish view of Samaritans 1990:53-58), referring to them in such positive terms certainly represented a new or modified social perspective which could easily have been understood to include Gentiles.

Luke 15:11-32

Another hint may be in the story of the Prodigal Son (Lk.15:11-32). The son lives among Gentiles, sinking to the lowest depths a Jew can reach. Yet when he returns home in a penitent spirit his father receives him. Having had contact with Gentiles did not place him beyond the loving embrace of his father.

The Universal Scope of God's Plan Revealed and Set in Motion

Luke 24:45-49

It is not until the end of volume one that Luke specifically reveals the universal scope of God's plan. Just before recording Jesus' ascension back to heaven, Luke records Jesus' commission to his followers:

> *Then he opened their minds to understand these many Scriptures. And he said, Yes, it was written long ago that the Messiah must suffer and die and rise again from the dead on the third day. With my authority, take this message of repentance to all the nations, beginning in Jerusalem: There is forgiveness of sins for all who turn to me. You are witnesses of all these things.*
> *And now I will send the Holy Spirit, just as my Father promised. But stay here in the city until the Holy Spirit comes and fills you with power from heaven* (Lk. 24:45-49).

They are to take the message of repentance and forgiveness of sins to *all the nations* (*pánta tá éthna*). Luke uses the same phrase as does Matthew, the meaning of which cannot be mistaken. *All the nations* means Gentiles. The command is clearly universal in scope. Nissen notes that this mission, which finds it roots in a suffering messiah and includes all people, is based on a re-reading (a re-interpretation) of Scripture (1999:50). Jesus opened their minds, enabling them to see things from a new perspective. Not only must they understand the messiah differently than they have in the past, they must think about other people differently than they have in the past. Each of these will require that they rethink, reinterpret, and reapply the Scriptures.

We do not know how much time elapsed between Theophilus' receiving Luke's first book and his second. To provide a time-frame for Theophilus and set the stage for the events that would follow, Luke's opening section of Acts overlaps the closing section of his Gospel. Jesus' followers are to wait in Jerusalem until they are empowered by the Holy Spirit. When they are, they will begin their witnessing ministry that will radiate out from Jerusalem to Judea, to Samaria, and to the ends of the earth. To *the ends of the earth* in Acts is equal to *all the nations* in the Gospel (Wall 2002:Vol. 10, 42).

The universality of God's plan is unmistakable—at least from our perspective. Whether or not that first generation of Jewish believers fully understood the universality of God's plan is open to discussion. If they understood, why did they not obey? It was approximately ten years before Gentiles finally had an opportunity to hear and respond to the gospel. Why did it take so long? Was the reality of what God wanted simply too much for the Jewish mind to comprehend and act on? Or did they understand and simply fail to obey? There is no way to answer the question definitively. Perhaps it simply took a while for them to get to a place in their spiritual and emotional maturity to be able to actually do what they knew God expected them to do.

Acts 2:39

Luke's next reference to the universal scope of God's plan comes in Peter's sermon when, in Acts 2:39, he refers to all those who are *far away*. Is this a reference to Gentiles, or could it simply refer to Jews of the Diaspora? Bruce and Larkin both link Peter's words to Isaiah 57:19, where God promises to heal those who are *"far and near,"* (Bruce 1954:78, Larkin 1995:59). Kidner, commenting on the Isaiah text, sees it as the basis for Paul's comments in Ephesians 2:11-18 (1994: 665), where it is clear that he is speaking of Gentiles. The general consensus among scholars is that Peter is referring to Gentiles. Thus, Peter affirms the universality of God's plan—whether or not he is spiritually and emotionally mature enough to act on it at the time.

Acts 3:12-26

Luke's next reference to the universality of God's plan comes in Peter's sermon recorded in Ac.3:12-26. In verse 25, Peter refers to Genesis 22:18 and God's promise to bless all the people (or *nations*) of the earth. Even if the Isaiah reference (57:19) noted above may seem somewhat vague regarding the Gentiles, this reference is not. God's original promise to Abraham included all people, not only Abraham's descendants. All the necessary events had occurred and God was fulfilling his promise to Abraham, a promise that included *all people*.

Acts 6:5

Another reference that may be linked to the universal theme in Acts is found in 6:5. It is a minor theme and may fit better into the category of "hints" rather than an outright statement, but Luke's notation that Nicolas is a proselyte, that is, a Gentile who converted to Judaism, is interesting. The door had always been open for Gentiles who wished to become part of the Israelite community. Perhaps Luke's casual mention of Nicolas' ethnic origins is designed to remind his Jewish readers that the inclusion of Gentiles among God's people has always been a reality—even if they were a very small minority.

Acts 8:4-25

The next step in the movement of God's plan from particular to universal comes in Acts 8. Philip travels to Samaria where he preaches to the people of a local village. Many of the residents are converted and the church in Jerusalem sends Peter and John to acknowledge and strengthen the new believers. Though the Samaritans were not highly regarded, they were not thought of as Gentiles (Dollar 1990:53-58). Preaching to them, however, did represent the crossing of a major social boundary. Perhaps taking the gospel to the Samaritans represented a halfway step in the movement from particular to universal.

Acts 8:26-39

Right on the heels of Philip's work in Samaria is his encounter with the man from Ethiopia (8:26-39). The text does not inform us as to the man's exact religious standing, whether he was a God-fearer or a proselyte. Bruce concludes that he was a God-fearer (1954:186). Either way, he was not a Jew by birth. If he was not a proselyte, but only a God-fearer, Luke is taking his Jewish readers one step closer to direct contact with Gentile people. God-fearers have typically been understood as Gentile people, who, though not fully proselytized, have embraced Judaism. They were allowed to worship in Jerusalem, but with restrictions. Scot McKnight, however, suggests that the latest research indicates that there may have been less a distinction between proselytes and Godfearers than previously thought (2000:835-847). Even if that is the case and the man from Ethiopia was considered a proselyte, welcomed (to a degree) into the community of Israel, he was still not really one of them. His access to the temple was restricted. Yet the gospel was extended to him. The new community of faith described by Luke in the book of Acts is open to everyone.

Acts 9:15

Saul's conversion in Acts 9 is the next step toward a full blown presentation of universalism in Luke's narrative. The specific reference comes when God speaks to Ananias (vs. 15), explaining that Saul was to be his (God's) instrument to take the gospel to Gentiles, to kings and to the people of Israel. The movement toward universalism becomes more specific as God selects someone specifically designated to work among non-Jewish people.

Acts 10

As far as the movement from a particular to a universal context is concerned, Acts 10 is the focal point in Luke's narrative. Approximately ten years earlier Jesus had commissioned his followers to be his witnesses among all the nations. As I suggested earlier, because of their spiritual and emotional immaturity they had not obeyed Jesus' instructions. The Holy Spirit has been patient but he can wait no longer. The time for action has come. Jewish believers need to move out of their comfort zone and begin working among non-Jewish people. Peter will be the first to cross the cultural boundary (actually it was more like a vast and gapping cultural chasm) between Jews and Gentiles.

The logistical coordination conducted by the Holy Spirit to bring the parties together is impressive. An angel visits Cornelius with instructions about Peter. Then Peter is engaged with a heavenly vision designed to make him rethink his position on unclean (untouchable) people. God uses clean and unclean food to make his point. The issue, however, is not food, but people. While God had previously restricted contact with non-Jewish people, those restrictions (which had existed in a specific context for a specific purpose) had been lifted. There were no longer any untouchable people. Jewish believers had to get comfortable with this and get on with what Jesus had asked them to do.

While Peter ponders the meaning and application of the vision, he receives specific instructions regarding the men who have come seeking him. He is to go with them. As Peter left to go with the Roman soldiers who had come seeking him, one wonders if he recalled Jesus' willingness to go to the home of the Roman soldier whose servant was sick. By the time Peter arrived at Cornelius' home he had figured out what God was saying to him—there were no unclean, untouchable people. When Jesus had said *all nations* he meant *all nations*, all ethnic groups.

It is interesting that although God had selected Saul to be the one to focus his energies on proclamation to the Gentiles, it was Peter who was chosen to be the first to cross the cultural gulf between Jews and Gentiles. I suspect this was a strategic move on God's part. Gentile inclusion in the Jewish community of faith would be easier for some Jewish believers to accept if it was initiated by someone like Peter— a respected Jewish believer, a leader who had been a member of Jesus' inner circle, rather than someone like Saul (Paul), who came to be thought of by some as a renegade troublemaker.

Peter himself may have ended up being thought of as something of renegade and perhaps a troublemaker for having opened the door for Gentile participation in the Jewish community of faith. It is interesting to note that after Peter reports back to the church leaders in Jerusalem, even though they are convinced that he did the right thing (Ac.11:1-18), he no longer appears to enjoy the position of leadership in Jerusalem he had previously enjoyed. Peter basically disappears from the Acts narrative. James

29

eventually became the dominant personality in the Jerusalem church.

Why was bringing Gentiles into the community of faith so difficult for the Jews to accept? There were two reasons. First, anti-Gentile thinking ran so deep among the Jewish people that the thought of associating with Gentiles was repulsive to many of them—even if the association was only indirect by allowing them to be identified with the community of faith. Second, the Jews believed the way they expressed and lived out their faith was the only acceptable way for one to express and live out his or her faith. For all practical purposes (though they may not have articulated their thinking in these terms), the Jews felt that their culture was the divinely appointed culture and that in order to please God one had to live as they lived. Or, to put it another way, their way of life, their *cultural forms*, were rooted in the Law of Moses. They lived as they lived because God had given them his law. To live in obedience to God was to live as they lived—so they thought (Kraft 1979:108).

Peter's response to the vision from God on the roof of Simon's house was probably indicative of the response of many Jews to the inclusion of Gentiles into the community of faith. When, in the vision, God told Peter to kill and eat one of the "unclean" animals that stood before him, Peter refused. He refused a direct command from God three times! That is amazing. But that is how deeply ingrained his beliefs and behaviors were. Learning to think and behave differently was not easy for Peter, even when instructions to do so came directly from God. For the Jews to learn to think differently about non-Jewish people was not easy for them.

Once the floodgate was open, waves of Gentiles came pouring into the church. As soon as Luke finishes his narrative about the church in Jerusalem questioning Peter's behavior regarding Cornelius, he tells of Jewish believers from Cyprus and Cyrene going to Antioch preaching to non-Jewish people. It is significant to note that beyond Peter, the first Jews in Luke's narrative to bring Gentiles into the community of faith are not Palestinian, but Hellenistic Jews. Perhaps for them the step across the sociocultural boundary between themselves and the Hellenists was smaller. As Ralph Winter and Bruce Koch have pointed out, the less the cultural distance there is between the evangelist and the potential convert, the easier it is to cross the distance (1999:509-524). Hellenistic Jews were culturally closer to the Hellenists than were Palestinian Jews.

Acts 13:1-3

Now that Luke has demonstrated the movement of God's plan from a particular Jewish context to a universal context, Luke will continue to demonstrate the universal nature of the gospel by focusing the rest of his narrative on Paul's work among non-Jewish people. Acts 13:1-3 is Luke's account of the Holy Spirit's call of Paul and Barnabas to begin specific, focused missionary outreach among the non-Jewish people of the Roman world.

Acts 13:4-14:28

Luke does not linger long on the call, but proceeds quickly to tell of their first extensive excursion as missionaries into the Hellenistic world (13:4-14:28). It is interesting to note that although Paul had been selected to focus his evangelistic outreach among Gentiles, it was not only to Gentiles. God had included Israel as well in Paul's audience (Ac.9:15-16). Thus, Paul always began his work among the Jews in each city. His practice, as he traveled from city to city, was to go to the synagogue, speaking first to the Jews. Of course, there would also be Gentile God-fearers there (Bruce 1954:263), which would open a door into the Hellenistic community. Generally speaking, however, only after the Jews first had a chance to hear and respond the gospel would Paul turn his full attention to the non-Jewish population.

Luke's account of Paul's journeys reads like a travel log, chronicling the movement of Paul's team from city to city, region to region, across oceans and land, in densely populated metropolises and small country villages, island seaports and centers of cultural, political and economic power. Paul moved confidently and comfortably throughout the Hellenistic world of his day. At this point in his story, the sociocultural distance Luke has covered is amazing. He has moved from the temple in Jerusalem to the larger Roman world. The distance in miles is not that great. But the sociocultural distance is astonishing.

Acts 15

Acts 15 provides a glimpse of just how far (culturally speaking) the movement from particular to universal has been. The community had changed so dramatically in population demographics that some Jewish believers (there is no way of knowing what percentage might have been involved) felt like things had gotten out of hand and something had to be done about it. From their perspective, Gentiles had come into the faith and had not been properly instructed as to how to live. The Jews who accepted Jesus as the messiah (shall we call them messianic Jews?) did not consider themselves part of a new religious movement different from Judaism. They had been Jews before they embraced Jesus as God's messiah. Now that they had embraced Jesus as the messiah they were still Jews. Nothing had changed except their understanding of the Scriptures in relation to the messiah. God was still the God of Abraham, Isaac and Jacob. Israel was still his chosen people. God had fulfilled his promise to send them the messiah. All people were welcome in the community of faith—but then non-Jewish people had always been able to accept *Yahweh*, the

God of Israel, as the one true God and worship him as part of the community of Israel. The problem, as far as some of the Jewish believers were concerned, was that the Gentiles were not being instructed in the Law of Moses. They were not being required to keep the law that God's faithful people had always been expected to keep. For many Jewish believers, this was simply an unacceptable situation. And this fellow, Paul, seemed to be the one advocating noncompliance with the law and the traditions. Something had to be done.

Representatives of this traditional Jewish perspective arrived in Antioch to address the issue. From their perspective, non-Jewish people who wanted to be included in the community of faith had to be circumcised. The issue was deeply divisive. The Jewish believers would refuse to have any association with uncircumcised people—including Gentile believers who had not been circumcised. As far as the Jews were concerned, to associate with unclean people made one unclean. Jewish believers could not go into the homes of uncircumcised Gentiles—even those who were believers. They could not eat the Lord's Supper with them (Bruce 1954:303). How was the problem to be resolved? The Gentiles had to be circumcised and obey the Law of Moses—in short, they had to become Jewish. Paul, of course, understood that non-Jewish people did not have to become Jewish to please God. He would not tolerate such requirements being placed on non-Jewish believers. The issue was discussed and debated in Antioch with great emotion and force. Neither side was persuaded. A church council in Jerusalem was called to discuss, and hopefully settle, the issue.

Luke's account of how the Jerusalem church decided the issue is interesting. First, Paul and Barnabas explain their experience of God working among the Gentile believers without those Gentiles having to observe the Law of Moses or Jewish traditions (culture). The implied logic is that if God is working among the Gentiles without their having observed the Law or the culture of the Jewish people, God must not require non-Jewish people to observe the Law and culture of the Jewish people. The argument is simple and eloquent. God was working among non-Jewish people who do not observe Jewish laws and customs. Therefore non-Jewish people do not have to observe Jewish laws and customs to be acceptable to God.

Second, Peter spoke about how God had originally accepted Gentiles into the community of faith without requiring them to obey Jewish laws and customs. Peter had been the one God had sent to preach to the Gentiles. The Holy Spirit had demonstrated God's acceptance of them without any aspect of Jewish law or culture being required of them. Gentiles were acceptable to God in the same way Jews were acceptable to God—by God's grace. The Jews had not been able to keep the law. Neither would the Gentiles. So why try to impose it? If God had not required the Gentiles to keep the law, Peter argued, how could the church?

Third, James then spoke, noting from the Scriptures[1] that God himself had said that the Gentiles would be included along with Israel in what he (God) would accomplish in the world. Given the fact that the prophets foretold exactly the events to which Peter (and Paul) had referred, James advised that the Gentiles not be required to observe Jewish law and culture. They should, however, maintain certain basic moral standards. They were to abstain: 1) from eating meat sacrificed to idols, 2) from sexual immorality, 3) from consuming blood, or 4) from eating the meat of animals that had not been properly bled. James (and the church) evidently felt that these concerns represented basic moral standards rather than specific Jewish cultural perspectives.

---

[1] Longnecker discusses the textual issues connected with James' usage of the LXX version of Amos 9:11-12 (1981:446-447).

It is an interesting list with far-reaching implications, the discussion of which is beyond the scope of this present study. The present focus is on the fact that the crossing of cultural boundaries had created a problem in the church which required attention, decision and action. As God's plan began to be that which he had always intended for it to be (universal), some of his people experienced a level of spiritual, social and cultural disequilibrium that caused them to react negatively. It is important to notice that the leaders did not attempt to address the issue by placating those who were upset. They determined proper behavior and then proceeded to behave properly, even though they knew a number of Jewish believers (possibly a large number of them) would be unhappy.

Acts 16-28

Luke's record of Paul's second and third missionary tours provides an ongoing framework for the presentation of the universal nature of Christianity. From Acts 21:15 to the end of the book, Luke's narrative demonstrates how the unbelieving Jews absolutely abhorred the idea of universalism. They hated Paul because he preached to the Gentiles. Even though the unbelieving Jews did not accept that Jesus was the messiah, the very notion that God would consider Gentiles equal to Jews (which is what Paul's work among the Gentiles implied) was repugnant to them. They hated Paul and wanted him dead. God, however, at least for the time being, wanted Paul alive. It was during Paul's trial that God's desire that Paul preach to kings became a reality. Luke's narrative ties everything up into a nice, neat package. God has a plan and it will be accomplished. The story begins in a particular Jewish context. It ends in a universal Gentile context. Why does the story end as it does, with Paul left in a Roman prison? It has an unfinished feel to it. Perhaps that was Luke's intention. The story is not over.

God has not finished what he is doing. The reader is compelled to wonder, "What will happen next?" That may have been what Luke wanted his readers to ask, "What will God do next?" Indeed, consider all that God has done since Paul was in that Roman house.

The Theological, Missiological Implications of Moving from a Particular Context to a Universal Context—For Them

What kind of theological and missiological implications existed for Jewish believers in the first century as the gospel moved from a particular to a universal context? It must be kept in mind, of course, that in the first century no one would have been aware of formal theological or missiological issues as we might think of them today. They would simply have been aware of problems or challenges related, in this case, to their understanding of Jew/Gentile interaction. We, however, can categorize and discuss the issues in relation to theology and missiology.

Theological Implications

Theologically, the implications include at least two matters related to hermeneutics: 1) a reinterpretation of the scope of the Law of Moses—whether it was universal or particular, and 2) a reinterpretation of the nature of salvation—whether it is rooted human law keeping or divine grace.

Reinterpreting the Scope of the Law

When the Israelites reached the foot of Mt. Sinai after leaving Egypt, God spoke to Moses on the mountain, offering to establish a special covenant with the people— with the nation of Israel. They would be his holy nation, his kingdom of priests. They were the descendants of Abraham, whom God had promised to make into a great nation. Establishing a covenant relationship with his descendants, giving them a law to live by, which resulted in a cultural identity unique among the people of that time and place was, in part, how God fulfilled the "nation" part of his promise to Abraham.

God made the offer (Ex. 19:3-6). Moses relayed the offer to the people, who accepted God's offer. Yahweh would be their God, and they would be his people (vss. 7-8). It was a specific covenant between Yahweh and the people of Israel. The basic agreement was that the two parties, Yahweh and Israel, would be bound (obligated) to one another. The details of the agreement, the rules of conduct for each party, were designed by God. He would bless and care for the people if they lived up to the regulations set forth in the agreement, that is, if they obeyed the law. The Ten Commandments provided the basic foundational concepts of the covenant. The additional laws (possibly in excess of six hundred more) provided the regulations upon which Israelite society, at least in part, was built[2]. In short, the Law of Moses, that is, the commandments Moses received from God on Mt. Sinai, were the religious and sociocultural regulations of the covenant between Yahweh and Israel.

The crucial question is, did that covenant extend to people of other nations? Were the Edomites, Ammonites and Moabites, for instance, part of that covenant? Were they the special people of God, descendants of Abraham who were the recipients of the promises? Were the regulations of that covenant binding on people of other nations? If the promises of the Sinaitic covenant were not extended to other peoples, neither were the regulations.

---

[2] Much of Israelite daily life involved typical Middle Eastern culture and was not unique to them.

When God spoke of replacing the Sinaitic covenant with a new covenant (Jer. 31:31-34), he referred specifically to having established that original covenant with the Israelites he had delivered from Egyptian bondage. Those Israelites, and successive generations, were his holy people. People of other nations were not. And they were not subject to the regulations of the Sinaitic covenant. Like Melchizedek had during the time of Abraham, they could live in relationship with God by faith[3]. In addition to being people of faith, the people of Israel had a specific moral, religious and civil law which governed their society as the special people of God.

People of other nations could come into the Israelite community, acknowledge Yahweh as their God and become part of the Israelite community by being circumcised (Ex. 12:48-49). "Aliens" living among the Israelites were subject to the Law of Moses (Num. 9:14), but people of other nations in general were not accountable to God for the regulations of the Sinaitic covenant.

It may have been that the Jews of Jesus' day failed to understand (or forgot) that the Law of Moses applied only to Jewish people. Perhaps Jewish believers reasoned that if a Gentile wanted to become a member of the new "Jewish" community of faith that they were obligated to obey the law of Moses just as were "aliens" in ancient Israel. If this was their position, it was sensible and logically defensible. However, it was wrong. This is the conclusion Paul and the church leaders in Jerusalem reached. Gentiles did not have to obey the Law of Moses. The Sinaitic covenant had been between Yahweh and Israel. People who were not Israelites were not answerable to it. Besides, that Sinaitic covenant,

---

[3] Of course, even under the Sinaitic covenant and its attendant law, one's relationship with God was still a matter of faith (Hab. 2:4). Being right with God has always been *by grace through faith*. But under the Sinaitic covenant there were a large number of rules to obey which served as an expression of one's faith and willing obedience.

38

that had applied only to Israel, had been set aside, replaced with the *new covenant* about which God had spoken through the prophet Jeremiah. The writer of Hebrews quoted the Jeremiah passage (Heb. 8) to make the point that the Mosaic covenant had been set aside and was no longer in force. All the promises of that covenant had been fulfilled. That is what Jesus came to do (Mt. 5:17). Jesus did not abolish the Sinaitic covenant; he fulfilled or completed it. When it had served its purpose (when all the promises associated with it had been fulfilled—and therefore when it had been fulfilled) it was replaced by a new covenant, just as God had said it would be (Jer. 31:31-34).

Jewish believers were a long time in coming to understand this. It is likely that some of them never did. Paul did. The writer of Hebrews did. If the church leaders in Jerusalem did not, at least they understood that the Gentiles were not part of the Sinaitic covenant and did not have to obey it. This much is clear from Acts 15. The theological implications of the movement from a particular to a universal context required that the Jews reinterpret the scope of the law. They needed to understand that the Gentiles did not have to obey the laws of the Sinaitic covenant.

Reinterpreting the Nature of Salvation

As mentioned earlier, salvation has always been a matter of God's grace. No one has ever merited or earned salvation. No one has ever deserved to be saved. Salvation is a gift of God based on his grace, love and mercy. This is not only true for those who have lived since Jesus died and established the new covenant, but was true for those who lived under the old, Sinaitic covenant. They had a long list of rules to obey, to be sure. We, too, have some rules to obey. But obeying them does not mean that we deserve to be saved. Obeying the rules of the Sinaitic covenant did not mean the ancient Israelites deserved to be saved. They could be saved in spite of the fact that they did not obey all of the laws all of the time. Both Paul and the writer of Hebrews explain that God was justified in forgiving the sins committed under the old covenant because he looked forward to the death of Jesus on the cross (Rom. 3:23-26; Heb. 9:13-15).

Being acceptable to God was never based on keeping law. This is Paul's point in Romans 3-4 and Galatians 3-5. Perhaps it was Paul's insight into this reality that helped him realize that Gentile believers did not have to obey the Law of Moses.

Jewish believers needed to understand that obedience to the law never resulted in being acceptable to God. It did not for them; it did not for the Gentiles. Therefore, there was no reason for Gentiles to obey the Law of Moses or observe Jewish cultural practices. Jewish believers who understood this could work effectively among non-Jews—that is, once they got over the disequilibrium (which for some of them no doubt amounted to emotional trauma) of associating with Gentiles.

Jewish believers had to deal with at least two theological issues associated with the movement of God's plan from a particular context to a universal context: a reinterpretation of the scope of the law, and a reinterpretation of the nature of salvation. What were some of the missiological implications they had to deal with?

Missiological Implications

Two key missiological implications of universalism with which Jewish believers had to deal were *ethnocentrism* and *contextualization*. While these modern terms would have been foreign to them, the problems and challenges the terms define were as real in the first century as they are today.

Ethnocentrism

Ethnocentrism is "the belief that one's own people group or cultural ways are superior to others" (Wan 2000:324-325). It does not take a great deal of insight into the ancient Jewish mindset as revealed in Scripture to realize that they had a serious problem with ethnocentrism. However, it is also easy to see how they arrived at their conclusions regarding the superiority of their culture. God had spoken to them. He had established a covenant with them. He had given them a moral, religious and civil code by which to live. Their culture was, at least in part, based on God's law. As far as they were concerned, their culture represented the way God wanted people to live. Of course it was superior to all other cultures!

There were several possibilities those ancient Jews failed to consider. First, they failed to consider that God could have required them to live according to a specific religious and civil code without intending to imply that all people had to live according to that same religious and civil code. That is, they failed to consider that what God required of them may not have been what he required of everyone else. Second, they failed to consider that God could have changed his expectations for them and for others—if indeed God had ever expected all people to live according to the dictates of a single culture. Third, they failed to consider that their interpretation of God's law, and the resulting Jewish culture, may not have been exactly what God had hoped to see. Fourth, they failed to see that they, as a people, had been impacted by the cultures around them—that they were, to a degree, a product of their time and place, as are all societies. Whatever they may have failed to consider, the result was the development of a very ethnocentric perspective. And that perspective became a barrier to cross-cultural proclamation and the development of contextualized, culturally appropriate theologies which would allow non-Jewish believers to live out their faith in meaningful ways.

Their ethnocentrism became a barrier to cross-cultural proclamation in that they abhorred contact with non-Jewish people. They did not preach to other peoples because they did not want to be with other peoples. Their ethnocentrism became a barrier to the development of culturally appropriate theologies because they believed there was only one way to interpret and apply the Scriptures—their way. The way they lived out their faith, expressing their devotion to God, was, in their opinion, the way everyone had to do it. Even when Jewish believers were forced to accept the reality that God wanted non-Jewish people in the community of faith, they maintained that their cultural forms, their Jewish expressions of faith and right living, were the only acceptable forms to be used in worshipping and serving God. Their ethnocentric thinking is what led to the controversy that necessitated the Jerusalem council. It slowed the missionary progress that could otherwise have been made.

Not all first century Jews were so ethnocentric that they could not engage in cross-cultural mission and ministry. Paul certainly was not. Neither was Barnabas or Silas or other missionary minded Jews who worked eagerly and lovingly among the Hellenists. Hellenistic Jews (such as Paul and Barnabas) appear to have been more open to cultural diversity than were Palestinian Jews.

Just as Jewish ethnocentrism presented a challenge to be overcome in light of God's universal plan for his church, so did the need to contextualize the proclamation of the gospel and the development of culturally appropriate theologies of life and worship.

Contextualization

Dean Gilliland provides the best overview of what contextualization is. He says:

> There is no single or broadly accepted definition of contextualization. The goal of contextualization perhaps best defines what it is. That goal is to enable, insofar as it is humanly possible, an understanding of what it means that Jesus Christ, the Word, is authentically experienced in each and every human situation. Contextualization means that the Word must dwell among all families of humankind today as truly as Jesus lived among his own kin. The gospel is Good News when it provides answers for a particular people living in a particular place at a particular time. This means the worldview of that people provides a framework for communication. The questions and needs of that people are a guide to the emphasis of the message, and the cultural gifts of that people become the medium of expression.
>
> Contextualization in mission is the effort made by a particular church to experience the gospel for its own life in light of the Word of God. In the process of contextualization the church, through the Holy Spirit, continually challenges, incorporates, and transforms elements of the culture in order to bring them under the lordship of Christ (2000:225).

The ancient Jews, of course, had no concept of a specific process called contextualization. Some of them, however, were aware of the need to make the message they proclaimed culturally appropriate as they worked with people of other cultures. This is what Paul referred to in his letter to the believers in Corinth:

> *When I am with the Jews, I become one of them so that I can bring them to Christ. When I am with those who follow the Jewish laws, I do the same, even though I am not subject to the law, so that I can bring them to Christ. When I am with the Gentiles who do not have the Jewish law, I fit in with them as much as I can. In this way, I gain their confidence and bring them to Christ. But I do not discard the law of God; I obey the law of Christ.*

When I am with those who are oppressed, I share their oppression so that I might bring them to Christ. Yes, I try to find common ground with everyone so that I might bring them to Christ. I do all this to spread the Good News, and in doing so I enjoy its blessings (1 Cor 9:20-23).

But even though Paul, and others no doubt, did their best to contextualize the message to a Hellenistic audience, many Jewish forms of worship were passed on to non-Jewish believers. This is evidenced by the fact that even today our Western forms of worship are so remarkably similar to the worship forms of the Jewish synagogue. As Jewish believers carried the gospel into the Hellenistic world, they established churches that looked like (that utilized worship styles like) their Jewish churches back home.

A typical synagogue worship service included opening with praises and prayers, followed by reading from the law and the prophets. The reading was followed by a homily (some would say an expository sermon) based on the Scripture readings (Martin 1964:24-27). When Christian worship assemblies moved from the homes of believers to church buildings, the synagogue continued to be a pattern for form and structure. The physical layout of the synagogue became the basic blue print for designing Christian churches. For the most part, Christian churches were rectangle, with an area in the front where the speakers would stand at a lectern (pulpit) to read. Worshippers sat on rows of benches facing the front. This structure was essentially a reproduction of the synagogue (Edersheim 1994:228-255).

How does the Western church's similarity (in form and structure) to the Jewish synagogue relate to the issue of contextualization in the first century? Contextualization, in proclamation and in theologies of life and worship, requires that forms and structures that are culturally appropriate to the people of a given society be used in local churches rather than importing the forms and structures of the missionary's home church. Instead of leaving the forms and structures of

Jewish worship in Palestine and allowing new Hellenistic believers to develop their own forms and structures for worship, Jewish missionaries brought the forms and structures of Jewish worship with them. And many times they not only brought Jewish worship forms and structures, but also Jewish theologies for how to live out one's faith on a daily basis. Their ethnocentric perspective led them to Judeaize (or to Palestinianize) rather than to merely Christianize. Many Jewish believers failed to see that preaching the gospel to all the nations required them to sift the gospel through an analytical filter in an attempt to remove as many Jewish perspectives and attachments as possible so that all that came through was the pure, unadulterated gospel rather than a Jewish version of the gospel. Some Jewish missionaries, like Paul and his mission team, were better at this sifting process than others.

Unity

Even a cursory reading of the New Testament reveals that as Hellenistic people became believers, sociocultural tension between them and the Jewish believers became a factor in the community of faith. It was a matter of concern for Paul in his letter to the believers in the region of Ephesus:

> *For Christ himself has made peace between us Jews and you Gentiles by making us all one people. He has broken down the wall of hostility that used to separate us. By his death he ended the whole system of Jewish law that excluded the Gentiles. His purpose was to make peace between Jews and Gentiles by creating in himself one new person from the two groups. Together as one body, Christ reconciled both groups to God by means of his death, and our hostility toward each other was put to death. He has brought this Good News of peace to you Gentiles who were far away from him, and to us Jews who were near. Now all of us, both Jews and Gentiles, may come to the Father through the same Holy Spirit because of what Christ has done for us* (Eph. 2:14-18).

The blending together of people from different cultures, with different worldviews is always a challenge. Each group, because of their ethnocentric tendencies, is predisposed to advance their own culture. As they do, hostilities emerge. This is "natural." First century Gentiles were just as guilty of this as were Jews. However, Christians are called to lay aside "natural" behavior and behave differently, according to a higher standard. This is what Jesus prayed for in John 17, and what Paul wrote about to the believers in Corinth and Ephesus.

The movement of the gospel from a particular Jewish context to a universal Gentile context provided many challenges for ancient Jewish believers. The universal nature of God's plan for humanity continues to present challenges for believers today.

The Theological, Missiological Implications of Moving from a Particular Context to a Universal Context—For Us

The church today faces challenges similar to those faced by early believers when it comes to the universal proclamation of the gospel. The implications of a universal gospel encompass concerns that are both theological and missiological. What are some of those implications and how shall we respond to them?

Theological Implications

Ancient Jewish believers, faced with the theological implications of God's universal salvation agenda had to reinterpret the scope of the law and the nature of salvation. The church today also has some theological reflection to do in light of God's universal salvation agenda. Some of our theological reflection involves the nature of theology.

The Nature of Theology

What is theology? Theology is the human endeavor of reflection and dialog about God and spiritual things, about the things we encounter in Scripture. It begins in the abstract. We *think* about God. It ends in the concrete. We *live out* our faith in ways that are consistent (more or less) with what we think. The "nature" of theology, therefore, is finite and subjective—as are all human endeavors.

This is not a new observation on the nature of theological reflection. But it is a reality that sometimes, in a surge of ethnocentric indulgence, is forgotten. Because theology is finite and subjective, it is important that we avoid two extremes. On one end of the extreme spectrum we must avoid the idea that there is one absolute (Western) theology for everyone. On the other end of the extreme spectrum, we must also avoid the idea that there are no absolutes and that every theological suggestion is just as valid as every other one. Neither extreme is helpful.

Two Theological Extremes

Extreme responses should always be avoided. This is especially true in theological reflection. The two theological extremes discussed below must be avoided.

One Absolute Theology for Everyone

Western theology is a highly developed, systematic, detailed body of thoroughly argued philosophical and theological propositions and conclusions about God and things spiritual. Western theologians have spent centuries reflecting, discussing, arguing and writing about various issues. The reflection has been so deep, so ardent and so thorough that some (dare I say many?) Western theologians appear to be convinced that every alternative theory, idea, doctrine or position for every possible topic has been considered from every possible angle and that the conclusions they have reached over the centuries are THE conclusions. For many Western theologians the process of theology is finished. The truth has been organized and systemized and Western theologians are the keepers of the truth. Their responsibility is to teach it to successive generations.

Admittedly, this positivistic perspective, rooted in Naïve Realism (Hiebert 1999:37), is in decline. Yet in some circles there are those who still refuse to consider alternative perspectives.

Rather than believing that the Western view of things is the only correct or valid way to think about spiritual things, it seems preferable to realize that the truths God has revealed in Scripture will be viewed, understood, and applied in different ways by different people depending on their worldview and culture. This is another way of saying that each group of people will develop their own local theology for how they live out their faith. A *one-size-fits-all* theology does not work. It did not work in the first century and it will not work today. Jewish believers lived out their faith in ways that were consistent with and appropriate to their cultural ways of thinking and behaving. Non-Jewish believers were allowed to live out their faith in ways that were consistent with and appropriate to their cultural ways of thinking and behaving. There was Jewish theology and there was Gentile theology. They shared a common set of core beliefs about God and Jesus, but how those beliefs came to life in their cultural contexts differed—sometimes considerably.

Some Jewish believers approached the theological challenges of God's universal plan with the same kind of naïve realism that characterizes some believers today— thinking that their theological perspective was the only valid perspective. That sort of thinking was not acceptable in the first century and it is not acceptable today. We understand the Scriptures from our Western perspective. Our understanding and interpretation of the Scriptures is colored by our Western worldview, our cultural ways of thinking and doing. People from non-Western cultures may understand and interpret portions of Scripture differently than do Western people. They must be allowed to interpret and apply the Scriptures in ways that makes sense for them. Allowing them to do so demonstrates our insights into the nature of theology—that it is a finite, human, subjective endeavor.

No Theological Absolutes

One theological extreme is the idea that there is one absolute theology, one way of interpreting and applying the Scriptures that is applicable to everyone. On the opposite end of the spectrum is the idea that there are no theological absolutes that apply to everyone. In general terms, modernism, expressed in positivism, gave rise to the former extreme while postmodernism, expressed in relativism, gave rise to the latter.

Harold Netland has discussed the pervasiveness of pluralism and the subsequent relativistic thinking in Western society today, even among avowed Christians (2001:13-14). The pluralistic tendencies and expectations in the West have led many believers to accept the validity all religious expression, which amounts to a rejection of theological absolutes—which is an outgrowth of the general postmodern inclination toward absolute relativity. It is beyond the scope of this study to examine postmodern philosophy. A number of excellent works, such as Netland's, already do that. The point is that extremes in either direction ought to be avoided. It is just as foolish to say that there are no theological absolutes as it is to claim that Western theology represents *in toto* the theological absolutes that do exist—which is clearly what some Western theologians believe.

While the extremes of postmodern relativistic thinking should be avoided, so should the extremes of modernism's positivistic naïve realism[4]. The very idea of God having a universal agenda for his community of faith requires that we learn to think beyond the limitations of our own cultural perspectives.

Missiological Implications

It is not possible in this study to discuss all of the missiological implications that grow out of the universal nature of God's plan. Two crucial concerns, however, that impact how mission is done are pluralism and syncretism.

Mission in a Pluralistic Context

Western society has undergone significant change in the last forty years. It has changed a lot in the last ten years. As people from other countries migrate to the United States or other Western democracies seeking relief from social, economic, educational or religious disadvantage, they bring with them their worldviews and cultures—including their religious beliefs. The religious mosaic that has emerged in the West is representative of the world's 4,000 plus religious groups. To describe the religious reality of the Western world today (to say nothing of the rest of the world) as "pluralistic" does not effectively convey the vast array of religious beliefs and practices one encounters in a Western

---

[4] Philosophical definitions such as naïve realism are a product of modern Western philosophy. Though the label is modern, positivistic thinking is not. The assumptions of positivistic thinking are evident even in ancient cultures.

mission context[5]. The very thought of outreach in such pluralistic contexts can be intimidating. It may be helpful to remember that Christian outreach in a pluralistic context is not new. Ancient Rome was a hotbed of religious pluralism. Many of the Greek Olympian deities were still popular in the first century, even though some were referred to by Roman names. Among the more popular gods and goddesses were Apollo, Aphrodite, Diana (or Artemis), Zeus and Hermes. Along with this group of deities were the emperors themselves. There were the Eastern mystery religions (some of which still exist today), and Gnosticism and Judaism. The gods and religions of Egypt were also prominent in the first century, creating an even wider variety of worship options. The animistic context of the first century (the belief in spirits and gods active in the material world who needed to be appeased by sacrifices) created an atmosphere of religious pluralism that actually rivals anything we see today in Western society (Bell: 1998:123-151).

It was into this conflux of animistic paganism that Jesus sent his followers. It was not an easy context in which to suggest that there was only one God and only one way to successfully approach that one God. Yet this was the message they preached. As Albert Bell explains, the worship of the gods was more a function of the State than of private devotion. The goal was to curry the favor of the gods in economic and political matters. "The more gods a city worshipped, the better its chances of divine favor" (Bell 1998:126). Bell goes on to note that: "Given that mind-set, it's little wonder that the Romans had difficulty understanding the Christian position. The Christians were making a religious profession by refusing to worship the gods and the image of the emperor; the Romans perceived it as an unpatriotic withdrawal from civic duty" (126). In other

---

[5] Hunsberger and Van Gelder, along with Guder and others, have taken their cue from Newbigin and have written extensively on the need to see the West as a mission field.

words, that which made you a good citizen was worshipping as many gods and goddesses as could possibly offer the hope of good fortune to one's community. Failure to participate in pluralistic worship was anti-community, anti-social and civically irresponsible. How could people even think about embracing a faith that stood in such stark opposition to all they believed? As different as the Christian message was, as shocking as it may have sounded to them at first, many of them eventually embraced it because it made sense. It resonated with a truthfulness that touched something deep inside them, drawing them into a spiritual relationship they had never imagined possible.

That which made effective outreach possible in the pluralistic context of the first century was not the preaching of doctrine or the presentation of theology, but the telling of a story, a story of relationship, of healing, of hope, of peace—things the ancient gods did not and could not offer. Even so, the atmosphere in which the early believers reached out to their fellow citizens was antagonistic. For the most part, their message was not popular. They were not popular. But they were right.

The atmosphere today in which believers reach out to their fellow citizens, whether in a Western context or not, is often antagonistic. But if believers in the first century could manage the task, so can believers today. It is a matter of being convinced of the truthfulness of the Christian faith. The challenge is not so much rooted in what others believe as it is rooted in what we believe. The ancient Christians were absolutely convinced of the rightness of what they believed. They believed, so they spoke—with passion, with conviction, not to judge or condemn, but as friends offering a better option.

Mission today is not any more difficult than it has ever been. Contemporary contexts, especially in the West, may be different than they were forty years ago, but they are a hazy reflection of first century Roman society, where mission began and flourished and changed the world.

Avoiding Syncretistic Results

Syncretism is the blending of one idea, concept or practice with another. In the broadest, simplest terms, syncretism exists in nearly every area of life. When words from one language, for example, are borrowed and incorporated into another language, that is syncretism. In many ways, syncretism can be a healthy, useful practice. But when ideas from a pagan or non-Christian religion are incorporated into Christianity in a way that fundamentally changes the essence of Christianity or a Christian practice, syncretism is harmful and must be avoided.

Christianity must be contextualized, in both proclamation and application. It must be culturally appropriate for each social context in which it exists. But Christianity must remain fundamentally Christian. It cannot be allowed to become a religious hybrid through the process of syncretism.

Missionaries have always agonized over the dangers of syncretism, especially in pagan contexts. The dangers are real. The emotional and spiritual needs that lie at the root of syncretistic practices are also real and are not easily met by missionaries who do not fully understand or appreciate the worldview of the people among whom they work. But pagan contexts are not the only contexts in which syncretism is a problem. Our Western modern/postmodern context is just as susceptible to syncretism as any other context. Twentieth century Christianity lost much of its natural vitality due to a syncretistic blending with modernistic humanism. Christianity, interpreted and lived through the lenses of a rationalistic, materialistic, individualistic, anti-supernaturalistic Western worldview, has not been the powerful force it could have been had it not been so diluted by modernistic assumptions. The church of the twentieth century accomplished a great deal. How much more could it have accomplished had it been operating at full strength?

What has this to do with missions? Given the universal nature of God's plan for humanity, missions will always be done in contexts where syncretism is a danger. Contextualization must be thorough and complete, done in conjunction with local believers, slowly and patiently so that the process does not open the door to syncretism[6]. This is especially important in a highly pluralistic context, such as our contemporary Western society, for the features that can be blended into Christianity to change it can come from so many directions and can take so many forms.

Another danger has to do with missionaries who are themselves products of pluralistic cultures. Their theological blind spots may open the door to syncretism.

Unity as a Goal of Missions

Certainly the primary goal of mission is that the church participate with God in his mission in the world—the reconciliation of all people. Yet to be reconciled to God includes full and active participation in the community of faith. Enjoying a relationship with God includes enjoying a relationship with his people, being part of a living dynamic body that worships and serves God, participating with him in his mission of reconciliation. If this sounds somewhat circular, it is so because of God's intention. Reconciliation results in relationship, which includes worship and service, which implies unity of spirit and purpose. Unity within the community of faith—individual local communities and the larger worldwide community of faith—is essential if we, as

---

[6] Hiebert, Shaw and Tiénou explain the process of Critical Contextualization in their book, *Understanding Folk Religion: A Christian Response To Popular Beliefs and Practices.*

God's people, are to be as effective as we can be in participating with God in his mission in the world.

The issue of unity is especially important among people whose culture is rooted in consensus-based leadership and community harmony. In the West, we operate out of an individualistic, majority rules democracy. Fifty-one percent is a majority and we go with that. The forty-nine percent don't have to like it or agree. In fact, they can continue to work to sway majority opinion in their favor. This kind of individualistic perspective may be fine in a democracy where we argue for what we believe is right and stubbornly reject other points of view. But for people who are used to discussing an issue until a consensus is reached and then working together in unity and harmony to accomplish their purpose (which is the case in many non-Western cultures), the discordant voices of an individualistic democracy are confusing and disconcerting.

Western people are so fiercely independent and individualistic, that our personal opinions and perspectives are more important to us than the peaceful unity and harmony of the group. Given our worldview assumptions, this kind of individualism makes perfectly good sense—to us. Most of the people in the world, however, do not operate out of a Western worldview. They find our thinking and behavior difficult to understand. Our radical individualism has impacted the way we live out our Christian faith and has resulted in the division that exists the church today. It is why there are hundreds of different expressions of Christian faith. And it is confusing to non-Western people. Would it not be better to relinquish some of our stubborn, opinion oriented individualism in favor of a more unified approach, so we can work together more effectively to accomplish God's purpose in the world? Jesus prayed for unity among his followers. Should not his desire for unity be more important to us than our cherished opinions?

If God's plan for his church in the world is truly universal, is it not imperative that we be a unified body? Is it not the case that a universal church must also be a unified church? Should we simply give up on the idea of unity because of the stubbornness (sinfulness?) of God's people? Should we assume that we will never achieve unity because of the pettiness that plagues us? Or should we set it as a standard that simply must be achieved?

Summary

Luke's two-volume work begins in a particular Jewish context. The opening scenes are rooted in temple worship and priestly ritual, sacrifices and incense, angelic visits, prophecy and supernatural events. God sends an angelic messenger to declare his intentions. Promises are made. Babies are born. Events are set in motion that will change the world—all within the context of the ancient Judaism. But even in that Jewish setting there were hints that what was beginning in that particular context would expand, becoming universal in scope.

As Jesus began his ministry it was still in the context of Judaism. But again there were hints that a larger picture would soon emerge. By the end of his ministry, Jesus made it clear that God's plan was universal in scope. The book of Acts also begins in a particular Jewish context, but with the full anticipation of a universal application of the events Luke had described in his first volume. Luke's story began at the Jewish temple. It ended in Rome, where the emperor himself will hear Paul's testimony about Jesus.

The movement from a particular Jewish context to a universal Gentile context carried significant theological and missiological implications for the Jewish church of the first century. It required them, among other things, to reinterpret the scope of the law and the nature of salvation. It required them to consider their ethnocentric response to non-Jewish people (though that terminology would have been unfamiliar to them), the need to contextualize the message, both in presentation and application, and in the need for unity in a culturally diverse community of faith.

The theological and missiological implications of the universal nature of God's plan for humanity are just as significant for the church today. They include remembering the subjective and therefore finite nature of theology and the possibility of extreme positions: that there is one absolute theology for everyone, or that there are no theological absolutes. The missiological implications include: the reality of mission being done in a pluralistic context, as it was in the first century, the importance of avoiding syncretism, and unity as one of the goals of evangelistic outreach.

Chapter 2 will be a study of the Holy Spirit in Luke-Acts. For Luke, the Holy Spirit's role included inspiring witness, and directing and empowering mission.

CHAPTER 2

THE HOLY SPIRIT IN LUKE-ACTS: INSPIRING WITNESS, DIRECTING AND EMPOWERING MISSION

It is not surprising that Luke's presentation of the Holy Spirit does not amount to a formal pneumatology. As noted earlier, Luke's purpose was not to present a formal or systematized theology, but to tell a story. Luke's narrative is packed with subjects of theological and missiological significance which emerge slowly and naturally over the course of his presentation. One highly significant subject which emerges over the course of the story is the role of the Holy Spirit in the life and ministry of Jesus and the community of faith.

A great deal has been written about the Holy Spirit in Luke-Acts. It is not my purpose here to provide an exhaustive analysis of that material. A source that does provide a good analysis of scholarly approaches to the role of the Holy Spirit in Luke-Acts is Ju Hus's study, *A Dynamic Reading of the Holy Spirit in Luke-Acts* (2001). As Conzelmann, Shelton and others have seen in their own studies, Hur sees inspired or prophetic witness as one of the main functions of the Spirit in Luke-Acts. But Hur's

58

analysis goes deeper, suggesting that Luke's intention was to present the Holy Spirit as one of the "divine characters" in the story being told (279). Those who glorify God for what he has done or who witness concerning Jesus do so because they are "filled with the Holy Spirit." The Spirit's presence and activity lend credibility to the things that are said and done. Thus the Spirit's "character" in Luke's plot is vitally important to Luke's literary purpose. Thinking of the Holy Spirit as a divine character in Luke's story will be helpful as we proceed to analyze specific references to the Spirit in Luke-Acts.

References to the Holy Spirit in Luke's Gospel

Fourteen different contexts include references to the Holy Spirit in Luke's Gospel. We will examine each one briefly, making observations regarding the Spirit's activity.

Luke 1:15

Luke's first reference to the Holy Spirit is in a context concerning John the Baptist. The angel Gabriel explains to Zechariah, John's father, that John will be filled with the Holy Spirit even before he is born. Shelton notes that Luke uses the phrase "filled with the Holy Spirit" to indicate the reception of the Spirit, and to remind readers that the person filled with the Spirit speaks authoritatively (1991:5, 11). I would add that it implies the *active presence* of the Spirit in one's life. Luke is aware of the role John will play in the introduction of Jesus. He is setting the stage for John's authoritative witness as to Jesus' identity. It will become apparent that one of the key roles of the Spirit in Luke's two-volume narrative is enabling authoritative or inspired witness (Shelton 1991:5). As a result of the Spirit's active presence in a person's life that individual speaks authoritatively regarding God's activity, Jesus' identity, or other vital spiritual concerns.

Luke 1:35

In this reference, the Holy Spirit is associated with the incarnation. The Holy Spirit becomes the agent of incarnation by causing Mary to conceive. The Spirit is not a natural being, but a supernatural being. When he acts, his actions are supernatural. Because of his involvement, Mary's conception was not natural, but supernatural. The Spirit is the one through whom God's power is channeled. Also, because he is the *Holy* Spirit, the child conceived by his involvement will also be *holy*. Since the Holy Spirit "fathered" the child (from a metaphorical perspective) the child is holy. The Spirit's presence has a sanctifying affect. Because the Spirit is part of the trinitarian presence of God, the child will be the Son of God—God in human form.

The Spirit's presence in Luke's story is one of the things that makes it so compelling. The characters in the story are not merely ordinary people doing what ordinary people do. They are people through whom the Spirit accomplishes his purpose. Thus Luke establishes a divine connection between the people and the events of his story.

Luke 1:41

This reference concerns Elizabeth being "filled" with the Holy Spirit. Elizabeth carried a child of prophecy in her womb—a child who was to be filled with the Holy Spirit even before he was born. Mary carried the promised and holy messiah of God in her womb. As Mary approached Elizabeth, Elizabeth's baby kicked hard, which she interpreted as a leap—perhaps a leap of joy at the nearness of the messiah. Elizabeth was then filled with the Holy Spirit and praised Mary for her faith. Luke's point is not only what

Elizabeth said—that Mary had been blessed by God because of her faith (vs. 45)—but that she said it by the power of the Holy Spirit. The Spirit's active presence in Elizabeth's life enabled her to provide credible witness regarding God's activity in the events about which Luke wrote.

Luke 1:67

In this text, Zechariah is filled with the Holy Spirit. As a result, he speaks as prophet and witness concerning God's blessing of his people as his promises to them are fulfilled. Zechariah's insights are not only those of an Israelite priest, but of an Israelite priest who has been visited by an angel with a message from God, and who is now enabled to speak authoritatively because he is filled with the Holy Spirit. Again, the active presence of the Spirit lends credibility to the events as they occur.

Luke 2:25-32

This reference concerning Simeon is another where inspired witness occurs. Simeon was filled with the Holy Spirit and identified Jesus as God's promised messiah. But on this occasion not only did the Spirit fill Simeon, enabling him to provide credible witness, it was the Spirit who led Simeon to Jesus so he could identify him. The Spirit not only enables people to speak, he directs their movements, providing opportunity for inspired witness.

Luke 3:16

Here the Holy Spirit is introduced as one who will play a significant role in Jesus' ministry. Jesus will "baptize" in the Holy Spirit and in fire. What did John mean? Being baptized in the Holy Spirit and in fire may represent the cleansing, sanctifying impact the Spirit would have in a believer's life. Perhaps due to the influence of the Essenes in Qumran (Beasley-Murray 1962:11-32), water baptism was understood as a cleansing ritual. Water washed away impurities. John's insistence that people be baptized for the forgiveness of sins was not lost on his audience. They understood their need to be cleansed and forgiven. Fire was also understood as a purifying force. Just as impurities in ore containing precious metals are burned away as the ore is refined in the flames of the furnace, so the impurities of one's sinful life are burned away by the sanctifying presence of the Spirit, enabling one to stand in the very presence of God. In addition to enabling inspired witness and leading willing followers, the Spirit in Luke's story is also presented as one who cleanses, purifies, and sanctifies.

Luke 3:22

The role of the Holy Spirit in Jesus' life and ministry is of particular interest to Luke. This reference occurs at the baptism of Jesus. The Spirit descends on Jesus in a visible form and God speaks. Both signs (the visible descent of the Spirit and the voice of God) are intended to provide testimony as to Jesus' identity—his relationship to God. Shelton asks whether Jesus' reception of the Spirit at his baptism coincides with the believer's reception of the Spirit at baptism. He also asks if the descent of the Spirit on Jesus at his baptism was more than a testimony as to Jesus' identity. Was it also a divine empowerment (1991:48-49)? I believe the answer to both questions is, yes.

Shelton's question regarding Jesus' empowerment is highly significant. Could Jesus do the things he did because he was God incarnate, or because the Holy Spirit empowered him to do them? The question has to do with the divine-human nature of Jesus. Did the divinity of Jesus overshadow his humanity so that Jesus had special powers and could perform miracles? Or when the Word became human, did he retain the essence of his divinity but relinquish the power so that as a human he was no more powerful than any other human? If the latter, then from what source did Jesus' power come? The Holy Spirit.

As Luke tells the story of Jesus' life and ministry, he stresses an association with and dependence on the Holy Spirit that neither Mark nor Matthew include in their Gospels. This reference to the descending of the Spirit upon Jesus at his baptism seems conspicuously comparable to the reception of the Spirit all believers experience at baptism (Ac. 2:38). Perhaps Luke is intending to imply that Jesus received the Holy Spirit at the beginning of his ministry just as believers receive him at the beginning of their new spiritual life. Perhaps this is the first of several references intended to point to the Holy Spirit as the source of power and direction in Jesus' ministry, a source of power and direction that is still available to believers today.

Luke 4:1

If one removes Jesus' genealogical record from Luke's narrative (3:23-38), the scene immediately following Jesus' baptism and reception of the Spirit is his confrontation with Satan. Jesus is "full" of the Holy Spirit and is "led" by the Spirit into the wilderness where he engages Satan in spiritual battle for forty days. Luke's phraseology, *full of the Spirit* and *led by the Spirit*, indicates that Jesus was influenced and empowered by the Spirit. Perhaps Luke's terminology here sheds light on his comments in 3:22. The Spirit descending on Jesus at his baptism was more than testimony to his identity. It was an empowerment. Jesus is open to the Spirit's leadership in his life and follows his directions regarding a confrontation with Satan. How was Jesus able to withstand the full force of Satan's attack for forty days? Could it be that Jesus, filled with and empowered by the Spirit, was able to withstand Satan's attack? Could Luke have expected that believers who read Luke-Acts would look back to Jesus' reception of the Spirit and realize that the same empowerment and protection against Satanic attack Jesus enjoyed was available to them as well? In a narrative such as Luke's, one teaches by showing, by telling the story in a way that demonstrates the point one wishes to make.

Luke 4:14

After the forty day confrontation with Satan, Jesus returned to Galilee to begin his public ministry. As he did, he was "filled" with the Holy Spirit. Marshall understands Luke to be suggesting that Jesus was "equipped with the power of the Spirit" (1978:176). In other words, there was a progression of spiritual events. Jesus was baptized. The Holy Spirit descended on Jesus and God spoke to him. The Spirit filled Jesus and led him into a confrontation with the forces of evil, from which Jesus emerged victorious. Still filled with the Spirit, that is, yielding to the Spirit's leadership and strong in his power, Jesus returns to Galilee to begin his ministry. The clear implication is that the Spirit, as a divine character in Luke's narrative, is the driving force behind Jesus' ministry, providing both direction and power for what God wants to accomplish through Jesus.

Luke 4:16-21

In Luke's version of the story of Jesus, one of the first places Jesus goes after beginning his public ministry is to his hometown of Nazareth. The scroll of Isaiah is handed to him. The text Luke attributes to Jesus is actually a combination of Isaiah 61:1-2, and 58:6 (Stein 1992:155). Whether Jesus combined the two texts in his reading, or whether Luke combined the two in his narrative is impossible to know. Jesus said, *"The Spirit of the Lord is upon me, having anointed me to. . . ."* Jesus' interpretation of the passage in applying it to himself was that the Holy Spirit had "anointed" (called, selected, appointed) him to preach the Good News. The Holy Spirit was working with and through Jesus to accomplish God's purpose in the world. Obviously, Jesus considered the Holy Spirit a driving, directing, enabling and dynamic force in his ministry.

Luke 10:21-22

This reference to the function of the Spirit in the life and ministry of Jesus refers to Jesus being filled of the joy of the Holy Spirit. The joy Jesus feels from the presence of the Spirit overflows into praise to the Father for having revealed precious spiritual realities to those who have a childlike faith. The presence of the Spirit results in joy. Joy expresses itself in praise (worship) to God. In addition to prompting worship, the joy resulting from the presence of the Spirit may have also aided Jesus in his spiritual struggles. It is clear that there were times in Jesus' ministry when he was frustrated and disappointed with his followers. Satan, no doubt, would have attempted to use that frustration and disappointment against Jesus to create depression and other difficulties that could have given Satan an advantage over Jesus. How is it that Jesus withstood Satan's attacks every time, finishing his ministry without having yielded to temptation? Perhaps the joy Jesus felt from the presence of the Holy Spirit in his life countered the negative affects of the frustration and disappointment with which Jesus had to deal.

Luke 11:13

In this reference, Jesus speaks of the Father giving the Holy Spirit to those who specifically ask for him to be present in their lives. Clearly, the presence of the Spirit is considered a spiritual blessing, a gift from a loving Father,[7] available for the asking. Is Luke anticipating what he will write about in Acts 2—the Spirit being made available to all people? It is impossible to be certain. However, if Luke has planned his presentation (which I believe he did), he knows what he will write about. Like all good story tellers, he is preparing his readers for events they have yet to encounter in his narrative.

Luke 12:10-12

Two different considerations regarding the Holy Spirit arise from this text: 1) blasphemy against the Holy Spirit, and 2) guidance from the Spirit in defensive proclamation. Explanations as to what blasphemy against the Holy Spirit is are varied. Stein provides an overview of suggested explanations (1998:348-349). One explanation of the sin suggests an ongoing refusal to heed the Spirit's promptings to turn from sin to God. This reality, if it is what Jesus had in mind, is not, however, readily apparent in the text. A simple reading of the text suggests the blasphemy is saying ugly or evil things about the Spirit, perhaps by way of accusation. What is clear from the passage is the seriousness that should be attached to the Spirit's work.

As for the guidance aspect of what Luke records in this text, the Holy Spirit is seen as the source of inspired defense when disciples are required to answer charges leveled by persecutors. The Holy Spirit teaches, guides and

---

[7] Stein (1992:328) and Marshall (1978:469-470) discuss the possibility that Matthew's version of this conversation in which Jesus refers to "good gifts" may more closely represent the original dialog. Luke's reference to the Holy Spirit as the gift of God may be due to his theological emphasis. If this is so, Luke's thought may have been that of all the gifts God can give, the Holy Spirit epitomizes the richness of God's blessings.

provides inspiration when needed. He is to be taken seriously. Respect for his work is vital.

Luke 24:49

In this last reference to the Holy Spirit in Luke's Gospel the focus is on the Spirit as one sent by Jesus to empower his followers, enabling them to complete their assigned task. If the Spirit has empowered and enabled Jesus to accomplish his ministry objectives, the Spirit will enable Jesus' followers to do the same. Surely this was Jesus' meaning and the idea Luke intended to convey. The Spirit empowers for ministry. God's people are not left to flounder in a sea of finitude. Rather, they soar on eagles wings, lifted high by the power of the Holy Spirit.

Summary of the Activities of the Holy Spirit in Luke's Gospel

The phrase "filled with the Holy Spirit" or "full of the Holy Spirit," is used six times in the Gospel. Normally it is used prior to or just after some form of inspired speech. One additional time the phrase "filled with" is used to refer to the joy associated with the presence of the Holy Spirit. This (along with the material about the Holy Spirit in Acts which we have yet to discuss) has led a number of scholars to conclude that the main function (or at least one of the main functions) of the Holy Spirit in Luke's narrative is to inspire witness concerning Jesus. Inspired witness is certainly *a* major function of the Holy Spirit in Luke's narrative. However, in Luke's Gospel the Holy Spirit is also involved in sanctification. The Holy Spirit makes people holy. He selects and empowers, leads, guides and directs. He provides inspired defense and instills joy.

Ten of the fourteen references to the Holy Spirit in the Gospel are in the first four chapters. Why such a front-end load? Perhaps the idea of the Spirit as a *divine character* in Luke's story provides a clue. The majority of Luke's references to the Spirit occur in the beginning of his work in order to reinforce the idea that the events he records are driven by a divine agenda and accomplished by divine power—both realities reinforced by the presence of the Spirit.

References to the Holy Spirit in Acts

There are nearly three times as many references to the Holy Spirit's activities in the book of Acts as in the Gospel of Luke. The following brief survey will highlight the Spirit's activity in Luke's narrative of the early church.

Acts 1:2

Bruce notes that the probable reading of the original Western text implies that it was through (by means of) the Holy Spirit that Jesus gave his followers their commission to carry the gospel to all nations (1954:30-33). In other words, it was the Spirit that prompted Jesus to give his troops their marching orders. During his ministry, Jesus had made it clear that he did only those things he was instructed to do by the Father (Jn. 12:49, 14:10). How was the Father communicating his will to Jesus? Through the Holy Spirit. Can one conclude that the Great Commission came from the Father to the Holy Spirit, to Jesus, to the disciples? Perhaps. But caution must be exercised, for it is too easy to construct artificial hierarchies that are not reflective of the complicated interconnectedness and interdependency that are characteristic of the trinity (Jn. 16:13-15). The point is that from the very beginning the Holy Spirit was intricately involved not only in empowering but in directing the mission of the church. He was part of the trinitarian leadership team that selected, trained, empowered and sent the disciples into the world.

Acts 1:5

Here Jesus reiterates John the Baptist's promise that he (Jesus) would baptize people in the Holy Spirit. As discussed in the section concerning Luke 3:16, the idea is likely the cleansing, sanctifying affect the presence of the Spirit would have in a person's life. Baptism was understood as a cleansing ritual. Individuals baptized in the Holy Spirit were cleansed and therefore sanctified. But is the cleansing, sanctifying affect of the Spirit's presence in an individual's life what Jesus had in mind during this post-resurrection conversation with his followers? Or was he focused on another benefit of the Spirit's presence? Verse 5 does not provide enough information to clarify the question. Verse 8, however, does.

Acts 1:8

Jesus' comment here is that when the Holy Spirit comes on the disciples, that is, when they are baptized in the Spirit, they will be empowered to carry out their mission: telling all people about Jesus and the possibility of reconciliation with God. The initial audience will be the people of Jerusalem. But the news will spread all over Judea and Samaria and will eventually become known worldwide. How could this insignificant band of believers have such an impact on the world? Left to their own abilities they could not. But they would not be left to their own abilities. They would be empowered by the Holy Spirit. As the Spirit was involved in the commissioning of the disciples (Ac.1:2), so he is involved in providing them with the power needed to accomplish the task.

Acts 1:16

This text demonstrates the view of early believers in relation to the inspiration of the Hebrew Scriptures. The original texts in question, referred to by Peter in verse 20, are Psalms 69:25 and 109:8. As far as Peter was concerned, David, the traditional author of the Psalms, had written those words under the guidance of the Holy Spirit. The Hebrew Scriptures were not of human origin. They had originated with God. While Peter would have been looking forward to the coming of the Spirit as Jesus had promised (1:5, 8), he also felt that the Spirit was already leading and guiding by means of the Hebrew Scriptures.

Acts 2:1-4

In this text, the Spirit comes upon the disciples as Jesus had promised. This is the baptism in the Spirit about which John had spoken years before and about which Jesus had spoken only ten days earlier. Three physical phenomena are associated with the Spirit's arrival: 1) the sound of a mighty wind, 2) what appeared to be small, individual flames of fire hovering above each believer, and 3) those same believers being able to speak in languages they had never learned. As a result of the Spirit being *poured out* on them (vss. 14-21) they were *filled* with the Spirit, a signal in Luke's narrative that the Spirit is about to enable inspired witness—something Peter did only moments later.

Acts 2:17-18

Peter's explanation of the physical phenomena observed by the skeptical crowd is rooted in the Spirit's activity as prophesied by Joel (2:28-32). Through Joel, God had said that he would pour out his Spirit on all people, that is, he would make his Spirit available to all people. As God pours out the Spirit from heaven, believers on earth are baptized in the Spirit. Thus the out pouring and the baptism should be thought of as the same event from different perspectives. Supernatural results would follow the supernatural event. Men and women, young and old, would be channels through which God would communicate. Dreams and visions would be used by God to communicate with his people, who would then pass on the information they received in the form of prophetic utterances. As a result of the Spirit being poured out, all believers can be filled with the Spirit and speak on behalf of God. Inspired witness remains a key feature of the Spirit's activity in Luke's narrative, contributing to the credibility of the witness by his presence as a divine character in the story and an ongoing reality in the lives of believers.

Acts 2:33

Here Peter explains that the Spirit is given by the Father to Jesus to pour out on believers. Benefits of the outpouring are not discussed, though Peter does refer to the things the crowd has witnessed: the sound of the wind, the flames of fire, and the foreign languages. The more astute in Peter's audience may have listened closely for the prophetic utterances referred to in Joel's prophecy.

Acts 2:38

When Peter was interrupted and asked about a proper response to the events that had occurred, his explanation included repentance and baptism for the forgiveness of sins. The Holy Spirit, who was now available to all people (because he had just been poured out into the world), would be given to obedient believers as a gift from God. Luke's record of Peter's sermon does not include details of the kinds of things the Spirit will do once received by believers.

However, it seems likely that Luke's readers would think back to the kinds of things the Holy Spirit has done previously (especially in Luke's Gospel) and conclude that the same kind of activity could be expected.

The falling of the Spirit on Jesus at his baptism may have been an especially meaningful event since at the baptism of each believer the Spirit will be given to him or her as a gift. Is it too much of a stretch to think that readers of Luke's narrative would expect the same kind of activity from the Spirit in their lives as they read about in the life of Jesus? While we cannot know what they might have thought or concluded, it does seem clear that there is an obvious parallel between Jesus' baptism and his reception of the Holy Spirit and the reception of the Holy Spirit by believers at their baptism. I am not suggesting the necessity of identical results in the ministry of Jesus and in the lives of believers. But rather an identical source of amazing power designed to empower Christian living and mission.

Acts 4:8

This is another reference to being filled with the Spirit. In this case, the filling is associated with inspired defense as well as witness. Jesus had promised the Spirit would teach disciples what to say when circumstances arose which may have resulted in intimidation and anxiety that might otherwise have frightened Jesus' followers into silence. The presence of the Spirit, however, not only emboldened them to speak, but instructed them as to how to respond.

Acts 4:25

This text, along with 1:16, provides evidence of the high view of Scripture normative of Jewish believers. For them, when David or other prophets spoke they were not speaking from their own initiative, but by the impetus of the Holy Spirit. This is the idea Peter expresses in 2 Peter 1:20-21. Even though they appreciated the Spirit's presence in their lives and the kind of personal, internal guidance he provided, they believed he also spoke to them through the Scriptures. It was the combination of the Spirit working in them in a personal way and his guidance in the Scriptures that yielded the greatest benefit in their lives.

Acts 4:31

Here is another instance in which being filled with the Spirit results in inspired witness. After an unselfish prayer asking for strength to endure persecution, the believers are filled with the Spirit and speak with great boldness. The Spirit has comforted them, assuaged their fears and emboldened them to continue their witness concerning Jesus. Inspired witness involves more than assistance with *what* to say. It includes all that goes along with being able to say it—in this case comfort, endurance, faith and spiritual courage.

Acts 5:3, 9

These references to the Holy Spirit fit within the context of the story of Ananias and Sapphira and their lie concerning the gift they offered to the Lord. When Peter confronts Ananias about what he has done, he says that Ananias has lied to the Holy Spirit. This becomes one of several texts where it is clear that the Spirit is understood as a person rather than an impersonal force. One cannot lie to the wind, or to gravity or to inertia. One can, however, lie to a person, a being, an entity. In addition to lying to the Spirit (vs. 3), Peter also refers to Ananias' actions as "testing" the Spirit (vs. 9). It appears that Peter is suggesting that Ananias' actions amounted to seeing how far the Spirit could be "pushed" by sinful attitudes and actions before those behaviors resulted in a powerful negative response. Again, this is descriptive of a person rather than an impersonal force. But Peter's comments can be understood to develop the theology one step further. To lie to the Holy Spirit is to lie to God (vs. 4). The Holy Spirit is not only a person, he is a divine person. He is God (just as the preincarnate Word was God and the Son is God) and as such represents God in the community of faith.

Acts 5:32

In another episode of opposition from unbelieving Jews, the apostles defend their witness and identify the Holy Spirit himself as a witness concerning Jesus and his resurrection. By empowering Jesus' followers to witness regarding Jesus' death and resurrection, the Holy Spirit is also witnessing to the reality and truthfulness of those events. The early believers considered themselves to be working closely with the Holy Spirit to accomplish the task Jesus had given them. The Spirit was a gift given to them by God to help them in their ministry.

Acts 6:3, 5

The context here involves the church selecting men who are "full of the Holy Spirit and wisdom" who can serve the physical needs of the Hellenistic widows in the church. The implications of the apostles' instructions are significant. If the church is to select men who are full of the Spirit, the Holy Spirit's presence in a person's life will need to be obvious, observable. How was the church to know if a certain person was full of the Holy Spirit? By the evidence of the Spirit's presence—inspired witness, godly living, joy, spiritual direction, wisdom—the kinds of things normally associated with the Holy Spirit's presence. The consideration here is two-fold: 1) that the Spirit makes his presence known, and 2) that believers allow him to work in their lives so that his presence is obvious.

Acts 6:10

This text involves an incidence of inspired witness, focusing especially on the quality of the Spirit's assistance. His *inspiration* results in a depth of wisdom that is far beyond mere human wisdom. Stephen's opponents could not find a weakness in his presentation. They were unable to respond to him in any legitimate way. The best they could do was to attack him with lies.

Acts 7:51

Here Stephen refers to the act of *resisting* the Holy Spirit. The Spirit offers instruction, guidance, wisdom, joy, strength. But he does not overwhelm and force what he has to offer on those who do not want it. God reigns supreme as the sovereign Lord of all, but he does not forcibly impose his will on people. Jesus did not impose his will on people during his ministry and neither does the Holy Spirit in his ministry. The Spirit is powerful but gentle, easier to resist than one might imagine. Millions of people do it every day.

Acts 7:55

In this instance, being full of the Spirit involves a vision experience. Stephen sees into heaven itself. This appears to be designed to comfort and encourage Stephen as he is about to be martyred for his witness. The Spirit had aided Stephen in his witness regarding Jesus. Then, as Stephen faced the ultimate sacrifice for his faith, the Spirit was there to help him through the ordeal.

Acts 8:15-19

This is a difficult text and it is not my purpose to blend it into a larger pneumatological framework. Regardless of what may have been the case in other contexts, in this context, the Spirit's presence had not been manifested in the lives of the Samaritan believers in any physical way. In my opinion, the believers in Samaria had received the *gift* of the Holy Spirit when they had been baptized, as Peter had said believers would (Ac.2:38). Yet there had been no physical demonstration of his presence. When Peter and John arrived and laid their hands on the new believers, they "received" the Spirit, that is, the Spirit began to make his presence known by empowering them to perform miracles.

What is Luke demonstrating in the telling of this story? Perhaps that the Spirit can be present (received as a gift from God when one is baptized) without him making his presence known in any obvious way. However, when asked to do so (in this case by Peter and John laying their hands on the new believers and requesting the Spirit's activity) the Spirit did make his presence known in amazing ways. I believe this is what normally happens today. Believers are baptized and receive the Holy Spirit as a gift from God. But the Spirit may not make his presence known until believers invite him to do so.

Acts 8:29

In this text the Holy Spirit directs evangelistic outreach. He does not leave it to Philip to decide what to do. Rather, the Spirit instructs Philip, who obeys without hesitation. The Spirit's involvement in directing the evangelistic outreach is not surprising, since Luke credited the Spirit with having told Jesus to commission his followers to go and preach the Good News to all nations (see comments on Acts 1:2).

Acts 8:39

When Philip's work with the Ethiopian was finished, the Spirit physically transported Philip to another location. This is the only record in the New Testament of a person being physically transported from one location to another. Why did the Spirit do such a thing? Perhaps there was a time concern. Perhaps Philip needed to be in Azotus in order to accomplish something within a specific timeframe and ordinary travel would not have allowed him to arrive in time. But regardless of why the Spirit did it, he did it. Directing the mission and ministry needs of the church required (at least occasionally) that he do extraordinary things.

Acts 9:17

This reference to the Holy Spirit is in relation to the conversion of Saul. Ananias laid his hands on Saul explaining that he had been sent by the Lord so Saul could receive his sight and be filled with the Holy Spirit. Presumably, as Saul received his sight he was filled with the Spirit. He was baptized immediately, and soon after began the ministry to which Jesus had called him. It would appear that we should understand the *gift* of the Spirit associated with baptism, and being *filled* with the Spirit, which is normally associated with inspired witness, as two separate things. Both involve the Holy Spirit, but the two are not the same. One, the gift of the Spirit, has to do with the Spirit himself. He is the gift. The other, being *filled* with the Spirit, is an effect or a result of the Spirit's presence.

Acts 9:31

The *comfort* of the Holy Spirit is the subject of this passage. Barclay Newman and Eugene Nida suggest that since the word *comfort* often implies relief from sorrow, words such as *encouragement, assistance* or *help* may be better translations of Luke's thought in this verse (1972:198). The church grew because the Spirit encouraged, assisted or helped the believers.

Acts 10:19

In this text, the Holy Spirit not only informs Peter that men have come looking for him, but that Peter is to go with them because the Spirit had sent them. The implication is that Peter is not to worry about the sociocultural implications of Jew/Gentile interaction. The Spirit was involved in coordinating the logistical concerns of getting Peter and Cornelius together. Evidently, the Spirit was/is responsible for the logistics of God's mission in the world.

Acts 10:38

The reference to the Spirit in this verse is part of Peter's sermon. He refers to Jesus being anointed with the Holy Spirit and with power. To anoint someone was often associated with selecting them to do a specific job. God selected and empowered Jesus to be his messiah by sending the Holy Spirit to Jesus. As the Spirit descended on Jesus in the form of a dove, God was anointing and empowering Jesus for ministry. The Spirit was not only the sign of what God was doing, he was the channel or medium through which God accomplished his purpose.

Acts 10:44-47; 11:12-18

In these verses, the Holy Spirit is utilized by God to demonstrate his acceptance of non-Jewish people into the community of faith. The Spirit manifested his presence by enabling Cornelius and his household to speak in languages they had not learned. Luke's record in this context does not include references to the sound of wind or small flames of fire as it did in Acts 2. However, Peter recognized what happened and identified it with, or linked it to, the spiritual outpouring on the day of Pentecost (Ac.2). Thus the Spirit's role in this text is to identify and legitimize.

Acts 11:24

Here Barnabas is said to be *full* of the Holy Spirit and strong in the faith. As before, we must understand the phrase full of the Holy Spirit to refer to the Spirit's influence. The Spirit impacted Barnabas in such a way that his life (character, personality, behavior) was different than it would have been if the Spirit had not been present in his life.

Acts 13:2-4

The Spirit is once again presented as being intricately involved in directing the mission of the church. He informs the leaders (the prophets) of the church in Antioch that he has selected Saul and Barnabas. It is significant that as Luke records the event the Spirit speaks in the first person. The Spirit has selected Saul and Barnabas. It must be remembered, however, that in 9:15 the Lord (Jesus) refers to Saul as *his* chosen instrument. In his own writing, Paul refers to having been selected by God (meaning the Father, 2 Cor.1:1). Far from considering these texts as contradictory or confusing, they should be understood as complementary, demonstrating the unity of the trinity. In many instances, that which is attributed to one expression or manifestation of God (to the Father, for instance) is also attributed to another expression or manifestation of God (that is, to the Son or to the Spirit). As Luke portrays the Spirit in this text, he is the one who selected Saul and Barnabas. The Spirit also sent them on their way (vs. 4), which would include enabling and empowering them for ministry.

Acts 13:9

In this text, the Spirit is portrayed as enabling Saul to respond powerfully in a confrontational way to evil opposition. The power to accomplish mission must include the power to withstand the forces of evil that oppose the spread of the Good News. Notice that while Saul is filled with the Holy Spirit in opposing Elymas, it is the hand of the Lord meeting out the punishment. Again there is overlap between activity credited to the Spirit and to Jesus.

Acts 13:52

This brief reference is to the believers in Antioch of Pisidia being filled with joy and with the Holy Spirit. The full impact of Luke's comment, however, emerges from the larger context of the events that occurred in the city. The unbelieving Jews of the city stirred up the Gentile civic leaders and prominent (wealthy) women against Paul and Barnabas who, as a result, were run out of town. In the midst of tremendous cultural, political and economic upheaval the new believers were filled with joy. That is not the emotion one would normally feel in the midst of such turmoil. Surely it can only be credited to the presence of the Holy Spirit.

Acts 15:8

Here Peter is recounting the events that occurred at Cornelius' house. The Holy Spirit manifested himself on that occasion just as he had in Jerusalem on Pentecost, thus signifying that non-Jewish people (who did not keep the Law of Moses) were acceptable to God. The Spirit's presence and empowerment were a sign of God's approval.

Acts 15:28

This is a significant text concerning the role of the Holy Spirit in Luke's narrative for it reveals that the church leaders were aware of the Spirit guiding them in decisions. Their comment, "*it seemed good to the Holy Spirit and to us to lay no greater burden on you,*" seems to indicate that they considered the Spirit a partner in a process rather than a dominant force. They were working with the Spirit to accomplish the task of leadership. They were not mindless automatons, but were God's human partners working with the Spirit in the oversight of his spiritual community.

Acts 16:6-7

While church leaders worked with the Spirit to accomplish God's purpose (Ac. 15:28), they were still submissive to his will. In this text, the Spirit instructs Paul and his mission team as to where not to go as well as where they should go. The Spirit leads, guides and directs the mission efforts of the church—that is, if the church will allow him to.

Acts 19:2-6

Here the Spirit's role seems to be that of an indicator or signifier of connection to Jesus. It is Jesus who will baptize believers in the Holy Spirit, or pour him out upon them. The believers in Ephesus had experienced John's baptism rather than baptism in Jesus' name. On the day of Pentecost, John's baptism, which was not rooted in the death and resurrection of Jesus—for those events had not yet occurred, was superseded by baptism into Jesus, a baptism rooted in his death and resurrection. The distinction may appear insignificant to some, but it was not insignificant to Paul or the Spirit. Since the "believers" in Ephesus had not been spiritually connected to Jesus by baptism in his name or by his authority, they had not received the Holy Spirit as a gift. Paul knew immediately that if these believers had not received the Spirit, their baptism was questionable. Obviously there is a link between water baptism and full connection to or relationship with Jesus so that one is prepared to receive the Spirit.

How does this observation fit with what happened at Cornelius' home? Perhaps the events at Cornelius' home should be viewed as an exception to the rule, since it was highly unlikely that Peter (or any Jewish believer) would have baptized a Gentile without some exceptional, undeniable sign from God that he ought to do so. If this is so, then the reception of the Spirit from the day of Pentecost onward normally followed water baptism.

Acts 19:21

This text presents a difficulty because the Greek phraseology technically may refer to the Holy Spirit or to Paul's own spirit (Newman and Nida 1972:370). Translators are divided over the issue. I believe that Luke is referring to the Holy Spirit. To suggest that the phrase, *"Paul, in the spirit,"* is simply a way of saying that Paul made up his mind to go to Macedonia seems to miss the point. Luke has already normalized the idea that the Holy Spirit leads believers in accomplishing God's mission. I believe this text is another example of the Spirit leading those who are willing to follow. The *"s"* in spirit in should be capitalized—*Spirit*.

Acts 20:22-23

In the Greek, Paul refers to being *bound in the spirit*. Most scholars consider this to mean *in obedience to the Spirit* or *compelled by the Spirit* (Newman and Nida 1972:

390-391). The idea once again is that the Holy Spirit is directing Paul's movements. In addition, the Spirit explained to Paul that he would face persecution and prison when he arrived in Jerusalem. Informing Paul about the opposition that lay ahead was one of the ways the Spirit prepared Paul to endure it.

Acts 20:28

Here Paul refers to the appointment of church leaders by the Holy Spirit. Bruce suggests that the idea is not that the Holy Spirit specifically appointed them to their position, as he specifically appointed Saul and Barnabas (Ac. 13:1-2), but that the Holy Spirit had given them the gifts that qualified them to serve as leaders (1954:416). That the Spirit made them leaders by equipping them as leaders is certainly one way to understand Paul's comment. However, it would not be beyond the realm of possibility that he was more directly involved. Even if he was not, he is the one equipping individuals to lead.

Acts 21:4

The reference here is to prophecy prompted by the Holy Spirit. The message, however, was that Paul should not go to Jerusalem. Why would the Spirit tell Paul to go to Jerusalem (19:21) and then have individuals prophesy that he should not go to Jerusalem? Perhaps Luke's meaning is that the Spirit told the disciples what would happen to Paul in Jerusalem and the disciples themselves suggested that Paul not go to Jerusalem. Regardless of how one solves the seeming difficulty in the passage, the point is that the Holy Spirit is actively involved in the dissemination of information.

Acts 21:11

In this text, Luke describes the prophet Agabus demonstrating how Paul will be arrested and bound in Jerusalem. The Spirit revealed this information to Agabus. Agabus is not arguing for or against Paul traveling to Jerusalem. He is merely explaining what will happen when the apostle arrives. The Spirit provided information when, where and to whom he felt it would be helpful.

Acts 28:25

This final reference to the Holy Spirit in Acts concerns the Spirit as the source of prophetic utterances to God's people of old. The message Isaiah (and the other prophets) delivered did not originate with them, but with the Spirit. He communicated with the prophets, who in turn recommunicated the message to God's people.

Summary of the Activities of the Holy Spirit in Acts

Of the thirty-nine contexts (as I have counted them) in which Luke refers to the Holy Spirit in Acts, he uses the phrase *filled with* or *full of* the Holy Spirit ten times. As suggested earlier, most of the time one of these phrases is used inspired witness is about to or has just occurred. Thus, inspiring witness about Jesus remains one of the Spirit's key functions in Luke's second volume. However, to stop with that observation is to fail to appreciate the complexity of the Spirit's role in the life of the early church.

In analyzing the text of Acts to determine the Spirit's role in the life of the early church it is clear that the Spirit functioned in many different ways. In my analysis I count over twenty different functions credited to the Holy Spirit in the book of Acts. The following list is highly subjective and another researcher may produce a very different list. If nothing else, however, this listing of the Spirit's functions in the first century community of faith demonstrates the wide variety of activity engaged in by the Spirit of God.

In the book of Acts, the Holy Spirit:
1. Instructed or prompted Jesus,
2. Cleansed and sanctified believers,
3. Empowered and enabled believers,
4. Inspired the Old Testament prophets,
5. Initiated divine communication by means of dreams and visions which resulted in prophecy,
6. Produced physical/material phenomena which demonstrated his presence,
7. Is received as a gift of God,
8. Inspired and enabled persecuted believers to defend themselves against accusations,
9. Served as a representative of God—represented God's presence,
10. Served as a witness to Jesus,
11. Changed lives,
12. Imparted wisdom,
13. Imparted joy,
14. Directed evangelistic outreach and cross-cultural mission,
15. Accomplished physical transportation/relocation,
16. Comforted and encouraged believers,
17. Served as a signifier of God's approval,
18. Served as a channel or medium for God's power,
19. Coordinated logistical concerns of missionary movement,
20. Provided guidance to leaders,
21. Gave gifts or abilities which equipped individuals for leadership,

Again, any list of this nature is going to be highly subjective and subject to criticism. But I do believe it demonstrates a point: the Holy Spirit was deeply involved in many different ways in the life of the early church.

Analysis of the Holy Spirit's Activity
in Luke-Acts

As Hur has suggested, the Holy Spirit is one of the divine characters in Luke's story. He lends credibility to the witness concerning Jesus. But his activity is far from limited to the background. He is not merely a secondary character who assists the primary characters in accomplishing their tasks. He does provide assistance to believers. But he does so much more than that—and he does it as one of the primary characters of the story. He is the dynamic force that moves the story along. He is present at every critical juncture providing the impetus for change and advancement. He fills believers with joy and wisdom. He changes lives. He leads, guides, directs, coordinates, empowers, enables, signifies and instructs. He is both a gift that is given and a giver of gifts. The Holy Spirit provided a dynamic link between the Father and Jesus, and between the Father, the Son and the community of faith. The Holy Spirit was the divine connection between heaven and earth, setting in motion God's plan to reconcile all people to himself. He was that part of God that came to live in his church, to work in and among his people, assisting them as they participated with him in his divine mission.

Theological and Missiological Implications
of the Activity of the Holy Spirit in Luke's Narrative

There are three basic premises that seem apparent when considering the theological, missiological implications of the role of the Holy Spirit in Luke's two-volume narrative. They are:
1. That God's involvement with his church is rooted in his divine, and therefore his supernatural, nature. There is a large segment of the Lord's church in the West which has traditionally shied away from the supernaturalistic aspects of

God's relationship with his people. Perhaps this is the result of having bought so thoroughly into the naturalistic scientism (anti-supernaturalism) of the Enlightenment that pervades so much of the Western worldview. What we need to remember is that God is not a "natural" being. He is a supernatural being. While God created the natural world, he has not indicated in any way (by what he has said or by what he has done) that he has limited himself to natural methods when accomplishing his will in his world. The actions of a supernatural being are supernatural.

Some of us are so comfortable with the supernaturalness of God's activity that we wonder why it would even need to be discussed. And some of us remain so uncomfortable with the supernaturalness of God's activity in the world that we still want to distinguish between the miraculous and non-miraculous activity of God. Yet the Scriptures make no such distinction. God's involvement with his church reflects the supernatural reality of his divine nature.

2. That God will, through his Holy Spirit, lead, guide and direct his church. This does not mean that the Scriptures become irrelevant or should be relegated to a secondary position. Even a cursory reading of Acts reveals that early believers held a high view of the Scriptures, considering them indispensable for spiritual growth and relationship with God. Even though the Holy Spirit was very active, his presence did not diminish the need for the Scriptures. However, neither do we find believers suggesting that since they have the Scriptures they do not need the Spirit. Those early believers studied the Scriptures, using them extensively in their personal devotions and their corporate assemblies. Everett Ferguson discusses the significant role of the Scriptures in the worship gatherings of early believers (1971:81-91). Yet they also cherished the presence of the Spirit who helped them understand and apply the Scriptures. As he does for believers today, the Holy Spirit gave those

early believers insight into issues not addressed in the Scriptures. He gave them hope and peace. He comforted and encouraged them. God made his presence among his people known by the presence of his Spirit in their lives.

3. That God's mission in the world (to reconcile all people to himself) is overseen by the Spirit and will be conducted effectively when the community of faith cooperates with him, looking to him for leadership and empowerment. The world is God's, the mission is God's, and the church is God's. As God's people, our mission in the world is to participate with him in his mission in the world. He has already made clear to us what the mission is. We need simply to ask the Spirit to lead, guide, empower and enable us to accomplish that mission.

Summary

The Holy Spirit is one of the divine characters of Luke's two-volume narrative. One of his main functions is to enable inspired witness concerning Jesus and concerning God's activity among his people and in his world. But that is not all he does. One can compile a lengthy list of the supernatural activity of the Holy Spirit.

The implications of the Spirit's role in ministry and mission are far-reaching. He provides the impetus for accomplishing both. This is so clear in Luke-Acts that one has to wonder why anyone would undertake any aspect of ministry or mission without complete submission to and dependence upon the Holy Spirit.

In the next chapter we will examine the cultural issues related to table fellowship in Luke-Acts.

CHAPTER 3

TABLE FELLOWSHIP IN
LUKE-ACTS:
THE ULTIMATE CROSSING OF
SOCIAL AND CULTURAL
BOUNDARIES

The term *table fellowship* has to do with sharing a meal with another person. Specifically, it refers to the cultural and social intimacy associated with voluntarily sharing a meal with another person. To sit together and share a meal implies a sameness, an equality, a willing spirit of commonality and unity. A significant feature of early Christianity was the fellowship they enjoyed around the table. This presented no difficulty as long as everyone was part of the same sociocultural group—which made them, at least in the loose sense of the term, equals. But in a world where social and cultural segmentation created wide chasms between people (between slaves and masters, rich and poor, Jews and Gentiles), the sameness was lost. How was the intimacy of table fellowship, which was integral to community life, to be accomplished?

My purpose in this chapter is to provide the historical background necessary to understand the difficulty involved in Jew-Gentile table fellowship, to define the issues involved, and examine Luke's presentation of those issues in his narrative.

Why Table Fellowship was an Issue in the First Century Church

Every society has rules as to those things which are acceptable and unacceptable, clean and unclean. Such rules, even in contemporary societies, are rooted in ancient tribal life (Toombs 1962:Vol. 1, 641) and apply, among other things to, 1) food which may or may not be eaten, 2) activities in which individuals may or may not engage, and 3) interaction with people— relationships within one's own group and interaction with individuals outside one's own group. Jewish society of the first century had very specific rules as to what was acceptable and unacceptable, clean and unclean, especially regarding food and interactions with non-Jewish people. Since the church began among the Jewish people, their rules and customs regarding food and interaction with non-Jewish people became highly significant when non-Jewish people began coming into the church.

What, exactly, was the problem? Was it merely a question of eating or not eating specific foods? While the issue of table fellowship may at first appear to have been related only to food, the concerns extended far beyond dietary regulations. The concept of clean or unclean, pure or impure, ultimately addressed issues of holiness (Wright 1992:Vol. 6, 729). The following sections will include a discussion of the Old Testament laws regarding purity and the social customs that developed in Jewish society as a result of those laws.

Old Testament Purity Laws

Regulations regarding dietary concerns are found in Leviticus 11 and Deuteronomy 14. Leviticus 12-15 contain other regulations related to purity: purification after childbirth, contagious skin diseases, bodily discharges, and what to do with clothing or houses that have been contaminated and are therefore unclean. The regulations are very specific and make it clear that the whole matter of clean and unclean must be taken seriously.

Deuteronomy 14:2 provides a hint as to why Yahweh was so concerned with the ceremonial cleanness of his people. God had set them apart as his holy people. As noted above, the issue was not merely about food or other details of daily life, but had to do with being Yahweh's *holy* people. What they could or could not eat (or other behaviors related to purity) had to do with holiness. Those things reflected their relationship with God.

Jerome Neyrey discusses the matter within the framework of the larger social context. All societies have rules (social maps, cultural guidelines) regarding that which is proper and improper. There are specific social maps that have to do with food: what may or may not be eaten, how, when, with whom, and in what manner. (See Mary Douglas as well 1966:41-57). Violating those rules places one at odds with society (Neyrey 1991:361-387). For the Jews, violating those social maps not only put them at odds with society (with their community), it put them at odds with God. To be ceremonially clean was to reflect God's purity and holiness. To be ceremonially unclean made it impossible to reflect God's holiness and purity. If God was pure, to be impure put one out of touch with God. To be impure made it impossible to participate with the community in religious ceremonies and rituals. In other words, it prohibited worship. The rules regarding purity, then, were highly significant. One's normal, active relationship with the social and religious life of the community and with God was interrupted by impurity.

Jewish Social Customs Related to Purity Concerns

Anything as grievous as disruption of one's social and spiritual functionality had to be given serious consideration. Since impurity could occur easily (even without one's specific knowledge), and since it had far-reaching implications for spiritual and social interaction, the Jews developed their own set of guidelines (which became traditions) to assure that they would not inadvertently become unclean. Mark, in an explanatory note to his readers, refers to this in his gospel:

> *The Jews, especially the Pharisees, do not eat until they have poured water over their cupped hands, as required by their ancient traditions. Similarly, they eat nothing bought from the market unless they have immersed their hands in water. This is but one of many traditions they have clung to--such as their ceremony of washing cups, pitchers, and kettles,* (Mk.7:3-4).

The washings Mark refers to cleansed the individual of any real or possible impurity, protecting him or her from the spiritual and social consequences of ceremonial uncleanness.

Another step taken by the Jewish community to avoid possible contamination and impurity was an avoidance of table fellowship with 1) non-Jewish people, and 2) even with Jewish people who were not very concerned with purity issues. In Joshua 23:7, Joshua reminded the people not to associate with the Canaanites remaining in the land. Perhaps this reminder is in some way related to the issue of table fellowship. However, in light of Mark's explanation of the rigorous Jewish traditions related to potential impurity, a more likely reason for their strict thinking regarding table fellowship had to do with wanting to avoid any situation or experience which could render them ceremonially unclean.

Philip Esler discusses the fact that the Mosaic code did not specifically forbid table fellowship with non-Jews, noting that their concern in that regard grew out of the dietary regulations regarding clean and unclean food. But the concern was not only related to the specifics of diet and ritual purity. Elser suggests the larger issue at stake for Jews was maintaining their separate identity as Jewish people (1987:76).

Another illustration of Jewish concern for ceremonial purity (and all that went with it, as suggested by Esler) is found in John's gospel:

> *Jesus' trial before Caiaphas ended in the early hours of the morning. Then he was taken to the headquarters of the Roman governor. His accusers didn't go in themselves because it would defile them, and they wouldn't be allowed to celebrate the Passover feast. So Pilate, the governor, went out to them and asked, 'What is your charge against this man?'* (Jn.18:28-29).

As badly as the Jewish religious leaders wanted to do away with Jesus, they would not go into the "home" of a Gentile. From their perspective, just being in his presence (in a house or place where purity rules were not strictly observed) could render them impure, resulting in their inability to participate in the Passover Sabbath meal.

Thus, the unwillingness of Jewish people to eat with Gentiles, or with Jews not concerned with matters of purity, was an unwillingness to expose themselves to the likelihood of ritual contamination and impurity, which isolated them from full and unrestricted participation in the social and religious affairs of the community, and, if Esler is right, could eventually lead to such social and racial integration that their unique identity as a people could be lost.

What has this to do with the issue of equality discussed in the opening paragraphs of this chapter? The Jews thought of themselves as the "chosen people" who had a special relationship with God based on their ancestry and the laws he gave them. They knew God. They knew how he wanted to be worshipped. They understood what kinds of things were important to him and how to live and interact with each other, and with him, in ways that assured uninterrupted social and religious communion. Non-Jewish people did not understand such things. They were, therefore, as far as the Jews were concerned, unable to enjoy fellowship with God. They were far away from God and were obviously inferior. The Jews, however, were close to God. They were superior. Of course, even within the Jewish community there were those who were closer to God than others—closer than their Jewish brothers and sisters who were not so careful about ritual purity. Those who were careful to maintain the highest standards of purity were the superior of the superior.

These ways of thinking dominated the Jewish community of the first century. Many of them became believers and were then forced to wrestle with their attitudes of superiority and with their theology and traditions regarding ritual purity. It is in this context that Luke implicitly and explicitly deals with matters of table fellowship within the community of believers.

Luke's Focus on Table Fellowship in His Narrative

Luke broaches the subject of table fellowship implicitly and within the context of the Jewish community. I believe he does so intentionally, wanting to begin his presentation of the subject in a low-key, non-alarming way. He begins slow and easy. But before he is finished he makes his point forcefully and obviously.

Table Fellowship in the Gospel

In this section we will examine each text in which Luke records an incident of table fellowship. His goal is to demonstrate to his readers that Jesus was not as concerned with issues of ceremonial or ritual purity as the religious leaders were. If Jesus was not concerned with purity issues related to table fellowship, do Jesus' followers need to be concerned with them? I believe Luke's point is that they do not.

Luke 5:27-32

Luke's first scene of table fellowship is in Levi's home shortly after Levi has left his tax collection business to be a follower of Jesus. As far as the Pharisees and teachers of the law were concerned, Levi's guests included people (tax collectors and sinners) who were to be avoided. Why were they to be avoided? Because Jewish "social maps" had resulted in a stratified society, sharp lines of demarcation were drawn between those who sought to maintain the highest standards of ritual purity and traditional observances and those who did not. Their extremely rigid standards of who was acceptable and who was not had created a large population of social and religious *untouchables*. Yet for Jesus, those people were not untouchable. He interacted with them just as readily as he did with those who placed high values on ritual and traditional conformity.

While there is no reason to assume Levi's table involved food that was unclean by normal Jewish standards, the people with whom Jesus enjoyed table fellowship in Levi's home were considered less than acceptable company for a rabbi who, presumably, was concerned with ritual and traditional conformity. Levi's guests represented the crossing of significant social boundary. Jesus was willing to cross that line, establishing social and religious ties with people others considered undesirable (Heil 1999:24). Luke's point, I believe, is that Jesus' followers must also be willing to cross such boundaries, establishing ties with "undesirable" people[8].

Luke 7:36-50

On this occasion Jesus is enjoying table fellowship with a Pharisee named Simon. Jesus does not practice social discrimination in either direction. However, Simon does not extend the normal social courtesies to Jesus: a greeting kiss as Jesus enters his home, a servant to wash Jesus' feet. Instead a "sinful" woman, probably a known prostitute (Heil 1999:45), comes into Simon's home and washes Jesus' feet with her tears of penance, drying his feet with her hair, kissing his feet all the while. Simon assumes that if Jesus was really a prophet he would know that the woman was a sinner and not allow her to touch him. After all, if she did not practice rigid ritual purity (and certainly a prostitute would not), she would be ceremonially unclean. Contact with her would result in contamination and uncleanness. How could Jesus not be concerned about such important matters if he really was a representative of God?

Jesus was a representative of God and he was not concerned about such matters. Clearly, Jesus held a different view on the necessity of social segregation based on purity rituals than the view held by the Jewish religious leaders. Once again Luke shows Jesus crossing social boundaries, demonstrating that the typical religious interpretations and customs of that day concerning social stratification needed to be adjusted.

---

[8] This issue of socially and religiously marginalized people or groups of people will be addressed in more detail in Chapter 5.

Luke 9:10-17

In this meal scene, Luke describes a crowd of 5,000 men. Perhaps women and children were also present. If so, the crowd could have totaled 15,000 to 20,000 people. Jesus multiplies the bread and fish to feed that entire congregation of people. Acting as the host, Jesus feeds the people without regard to location or the specific population of the group. As to the makeup of the group, the potential problem of table fellowship (from a traditional Jewish perspective) is obvious: what if some of the people in such a large group were ritually impure? Their impurity would contaminate everyone else, rendering the entire event ceremonially unacceptable. Jesus was not concerned about that possibility. Could location have been an issue? According to Neyrey, it could have been. The idea of "social maps" related to meals included a *map* (rules) of acceptable places in which meals could be prepared and consumed:

> A "desert place" is unsuitable for eating because it would preclude concern for: (a) proper foods which were correctly tithed and properly prepared, (b) proper persons with whom one might eat, and (c) proper water, etc., for purification rites. A "desert place," a chaotic place which admits none of the principles of an ordered cosmos, cannot in any sense meet the requirements of a proper place for meals (1991:366).

Yet in this "improper" context among these "improper" people Jesus acted as host and enjoyed table fellowship with thousands of people. Luke is demonstrating for his readers that Jesus was not concerned about the social conventions of ritual purity. With the beginning of Jesus' ministry a new spiritual focus was being demonstrated. God was more concerned with inward purity of the soul than ritual purity of the body.

Luke 10:7-8

In this text, Jesus tells his followers to eat whatever is set before them as they go out on their practice preaching tour. They are not to worry about clean or unclean food concerns while they travel about preaching the Good News. Even if they were working only among Jewish people, ritual impurity was still a possibility if traditional concerns informed their priorities. Jesus did not want his followers to allow traditional concerns to impact their priorities. What they ate and drank was not to be an issue.

In previous texts, Luke has been more subtle dietary concerns—at least from our sociocultural perspective. In this text, however, he speaks as plainly as he can regarding table fellowship by having Jesus himself tell his followers not to worry about such things. Clearly, Luke has a point to make.

Luke 11:37-54

In this text, Luke tells of another meal Jesus shared with a Pharisee and teachers of the law. The food would have been prepared to exacting standards and the entire meal would have been the perfect picture of proper table fellowship—had it not been for Jesus' behavior. Jesus sat down to eat without first performing the ceremonial washing designed to assure ritual purity. As far as the host was concerned, Jesus' behavior was scandalous. Jesus, however, had a point to make. He knew the customs quite well. His actions were not a matter of oversight. Jesus was demonstrating that changes were occurring (or had indeed occurred) regarding matters of ritual purity connected to table fellowship. By his actions, Jesus demonstrated that external purity was no longer to be the focus of concern. By his words, Jesus refocused attention to matters of internal purity. Of course, internal purity was what God had been concerned about all along. The regulations regarding external purity in the Sinaitic covenant were designed to lead worshipers to an understanding of internal purity. Unfortunately, over the centuries most of them missed the point. Traditions and ceremonies related to external purity had evolved without much regard for internal purity.

Luke 14:1-24

In this story, Jesus is again (for the third time in Luke's narrative) enjoying table fellowship with a Pharisee. This man was a leader of the Pharisees and had invited Jesus to spend the Sabbath with him. The Sabbath meal was an important social and religious occasion. In addition to proper food prepared properly, seating around the table was an important matter. The guest of honor would have been seated (or more properly given a place to recline) to the immediate right of the host. If the Pharisee's intention was to honor Jesus, Jesus would have been given the place to the right of the host. If the purpose was to dishonor Jesus, he would have been given some other place around the table. Luke does not tell us where Jesus sat, but he does tell us that Jesus told the other guests not to seek the places of honor at banquets.

One of the people who most likely did not have a place of honor was the sick man. In fact, it is probable that he was not even invited as a guest. Depending on the exact nature of his sickness, he held the potential for ritual contamination. His presence there may have been tolerated only because he provided a "test case" to see if Jesus would heal on the Sabbath. Jesus pressed the matter, asking the legal experts about healing on the Sabbath. When they refused to answer, Jesus touched the sick man and healed him. He then sent him away, indicating that the man was probably not a guest invited to share a meal with the Pharisee and his guests.

Jesus touched an untouchable man without regard for ritual purity. His willingness to touch the sick man provided a powerful illustration of his lack of regard for ceremony related to ritual purity and table fellowship. But Jesus was not yet finished. His story of the Great Feast provides another illustration of table fellowship across social boundaries. In his story, when the guests who had originally been invited to the feast made excuses and did not attend, the host filled his home with the socially marginalized, the social untouchables that one does not normally invite into one's home. By his actions and his teachings, Jesus was attempting to remove the social barriers that separated people, preparing the ground for a community of faith in which social and cultural boundaries would not exist.

Luke 15:1-32

It may not at first be apparent that this text is related to Luke's presentation of matters having to do with table fellowship. However, verses 1-2 set the stage for Jesus' comments in the rest of the chapter. The Pharisees and teachers of the law criticized Jesus for his associations, and especially his table fellowship with tax collectors and sinful people. Jesus was crossing social boundaries that respectable people, especially influential young rabbis, should not cross. Jesus' response to his critics is designed to demonstrate that God's priorities are different than theirs. First, with the story of the lost sheep and the lost coin, Jesus demonstrates that God is so concerned about the needs of lost people that he is willing to do whatever it takes to help them. Second, with the story of the lost son, Jesus demonstrates God's willingness to accept a penitent child from any context, even a Gentile pig-feeding context. As far as God is concerned, none of his children are untouchable or unembraceable. If these things are so, surely Jesus is justified crossing social boundaries and sharing a table with the people God seeks to reconcile to himself.

Luke 19:1-10

According the Jewish social maps, Zacchaeus, as a tax collector, was one of the society's untouchables. Jesus did not agree with the kind of social mapping that would put Zacchaeus, or anyone else for that matter, beyond his reach. Jesus invited himself to be a guest in Zacchaeus' home—which was the same as Jesus inviting himself to share a table with Zacchaeus, for all hosts were honor-bound to provide food for guests. Before, after or during the meal (we do not know which) the tax collector repented and Jesus declared him a true son of Abraham. Jesus initiated the contact with one who was socially unacceptable, demonstrating that no one, even a hated and despised tax collector, was beyond God's redemptive embrace. This was Jesus' point and it was Luke's as well.

Summary of Table Fellowship in the Gospel

Of the eight scenes of table fellowship Luke includes in his Gospel, three of them place Jesus in the home of a Pharisee (7:36-50, 11:37-54, 14:1-24). Two place Jesus in the home of a tax collector (5:27-32, 19:1-10). One of the scenes includes a reference to the tax collectors and other notorious sinners with whom Jesus often enjoyed table fellowship (15:1-32). Of these six instances where Jesus engaged in table fellowship, three are with the social elite, three are with the social outcasts. Jesus did not practice discrimination in either direction. He would eat with anyone interested in spending time with him. One of the remaining two texts concerning table fellowship involves Jesus directing his followers to eat whatever is set before them without regard to ritual purity (10:7-8). The other text involves Jesus acting as host for thousands of people (9:10-17). The location (a desert place) precluded proper preparation which would assure ritual cleanness.

In Luke's account of table fellowship in the ministry of Jesus, ritual purity is simply not something Jesus was concerned about. In fact, Jesus' behavior, as Luke records it, seems specifically designed to suggest that when it came to sociocultural interaction, especially when it came to table fellowship, a change in thinking and behavior was in order.

Table Fellowship in Acts

The focus in this section will be Luke's presentation of table fellowship in the book of Acts. As in his Gospel, eight texts in Acts deal with matters of table fellowship.

Acts 2:41-47

This text refers to two different aspects of table fellowship: 1) the table fellowship involved in eating the Lord's Supper[9] (vs.42) and, 2) the eating of normal meals together (vs.46). At first it may not appear that there are cross-social or cross-cultural issues related to table fellowship present in this text. However, 3,000 people were baptized on the day of Pentecost. There were Jews and, no doubt, God-fearers and proselytes in Jerusalem that day. Luke mentions fifteen different locations from which visitors came to observe Passover and Pentecost (2:9-11). No doubt, people from far away places were among the crowd of 3,000 who responded to Peter's message that day. It would be

---

[9] Bruce and Fitzmyer, to cite two examples, conclude that Luke's reference in vs. 42 is to the Lord's Supper. Translators of the New Living Translation specifically refer to the Lord's Supper in vs. 42. Others, however, such as Larkin, feel that Luke is referring to a common meal. I believe Luke is referring to the Lord's Supper in vs. 42 and to common meals in vs. 46

difficult to imagine that all of them were equally concerned with the dietary traditions related to ritual purity. Yet Luke seems to be suggesting that all of them enjoyed unrestricted table fellowship on two levels—common meals and the Lord's Supper. Social and whatever cultural differences that may have existed were of no consequence in the new community of faith. This important point is made early in the second part of Luke's narrative.

Acts 6:1-7

While this text does not address directly the issue of table fellowship, it does so indirectly, or at least as a related issue. The difficulty Luke describes in this text stems from the prejudice Palestinian Jewish believers felt toward Hellenistic Jewish believers. Perhaps the Palestinian Jews felt superior to the Hellenistic Jews. If such was the case, what reasons would they have for such feelings? One reason may have been because the Hellenistic Jews may not have been as careful to avoid contaminating contact with Gentiles as did Palestinian Jews. How could they? Hellenistic Jews lived among Gentiles and had dealings with them every day. This is not to say that Jews living among the Hellenists did not practice ritual purity. Many of them did. But it may have been that many Hellenistic Jews were not as careful about ritual purity as they might have been. If this was the case, Palestinian Jews could have considered Hellenistic Jews as ritually contaminated. It may have been that the Palestinian believers did not want to have contact with the Hellenistic believers for fear of becoming contaminated.

Admittedly, there is a great deal of speculation in such interpretations. But since Luke does not tell us the precise nature of the problem, we are left to our own devices. Regardless of the exact nature of the problem, most scholars (such as Bruce 1954:127-131) are content with some notion of a social problem between Palestinian and Hellenist believers. If all the believers had gotten along at first (Ac.2:41-47), what lay at the root of this particular problem? Bruce suggests that underlying social tensions surfaced, making it difficult for the two groups to interact effectively (128). Bruce is probably right. The more interesting fact, however, is that the apostles did not attempt to force the issue. Instead, they asked the church to select men who could be responsible to and for the Hellenistic widows.

Perhaps Luke includes this story in order to call attention to the problem of cross-social and cross-cultural fellowship. At first, when feelings of excitement and brotherhood were running high, everyone overlooked social and cultural differences. However, when the tedious reality of everyday life set in overlooking the differences became more difficult. The apostles sought an immediate solution, hoping, I believe, the larger problem would resolve itself in time. Unfortunately it did not.

Acts 10:1-11:18

The best estimate (guess) regarding a time-line related to the events recorded in Acts place Peter's visit to Cornelius' home near 40 A.D., ten years after Jesus had commissioned his followers to take the Gospel to all ethnic groups. Ten years had passed and none of Jesus' followers seemed to have any intention of going and doing what Jesus had commanded. Why had they not obeyed Jesus? They had ample time and opportunity. Can ten years of failure to obey be explained away as oversight, lack of proper planning or failure to execute plans? I do not think so. I believe that they delayed going because they simply could not bring themselves to cross the social and cultural boundaries that could result in ritual contamination. Consider Peter's response to the Lord's instructions regarding the animals on the sheet that was lowered out of heaven, *"Get up, Peter; kill and eat them."*

"Never, Lord. . . I have never in all my life eaten anything forbidden by our Jewish laws." Peter may as well have finished his thought by adding. . . *and I don't intend to start now.*

How does an apostle of Jesus defy a direct order from God? What could possibly have motivated Peter to do such a thing? I believe it is difficult for contemporary Western people to understand the depth of Peter's repulsion for unclean food. He had been trained so thoroughly and had internalized the ideas so completely that even a direct command from God would not move him, even when God explained that if he declared something to be clean, Peter should not think otherwise. Fortunately God understood Peter's difficulty. He was patient. God repeated the vision two more times and gave Peter time to think about the implications.

As far as the implications are concerned, it seems that God's purpose was two-fold: he was not only wanting Peter to rethink issues related to ritual purity from a food perspective, but also from a people perspective. To help Peter rethink the issue from a people perspective, the Holy Spirit told Peter that some men had come looking for him and that he was to go with them. Of course, when Peter went down from the roof to greet the men who had sought him out, they were Gentiles. First unclean food, then unclean people! What a shock to Peter's theological system.

By the time Peter arrived at Cornelius' home he had worked through the problem (at least on an intellectual and theological level). So he was able to explain to Cornelius: *"You know it is against the Jewish laws for me to come into a Gentile home like this. But God has shown me that I should never think of anyone as impure."* Emotionally it was going to take Peter time to adjust—probably several years given the incident Paul refers to in Gal. 2: 11-13. It was going to be a long journey, but at least Peter had begun the trip.

As amazing as it was for Peter to enter Cornelius' house, after Cornelius and his family were baptized, Peter and his traveling companions stayed with Cornelius for several days, which would have involved an extended time of table fellowship.

Peter's decision to take other Jewish believers with him to Cornelius' house proved to be wise. Luke explains the reaction of believers in Jerusalem upon Peter's return. *"When Peter arrived back in Jerusalem, some of the Jewish believers criticized him. 'You entered the home of Gentiles and even ate with them!' they said."* The other Jews who had accompanied Peter to Cornelius' home could testify along with Peter as to what God had done in that Gentile home. And though Luke makes it clear that in the end the Jewish believers rejoiced that God had opened the doors of the kingdom to non-Jewish people, it is difficult to imagine that they did not have mixed feelings about it. It was one thing for them to acknowledge that the Gentiles could come into the community of faith. It was quite another to openly embrace them as equals, enjoying with them the intimacy of table fellowship[10].

This text regarding the inclusion of Gentiles into the community of faith is one of the most crucial features of Luke's narrative after the death and resurrection of Jesus and the establishment of the church on the day of Pentecost. It is directly related to the issue of table fellowship and related questions of ritual purity. Luke's purpose for making it such a major focus is not only to tell the story of what had already happened, his purpose is also to encourage his Jewish readers who may still be struggling with table fellowship to rethink the matter in light of what Jesus did in his earthly ministry and what the Holy Spirit did in bringing Gentiles into the community of faith.

---

[10] This was obviously the case given the events of Gal. 2, Ac. 15, and Paul's emphasis of Jew-Gentile unity in Eph. 2:14ff.

Acts 15:1-31

We normally think of the Jerusalem conference in terms of the controversy related to requiring the Gentile believers to submit to circumcision and to keep the law of Moses. However, it is important to ask why the Jewish believers insisted on Gentile compliance to the law. Jewish believers wanted Gentile believers to keep the Law of Moses because as far as the Jews were concerned, God's people had always been required to keep the law. God gave the law to his people and he expected them to live by it. If non-Jewish people wanted to become part of the community of faith (the *Jewish* community of faith—which is how the Jewish believers understood it) they were welcome on the same basis non-Jews had always been welcome: they needed to be circumcised and live according to the dictates of the Sinaitic covenant. On the surface, this was their reason for demanding Gentile compliance to the Law of Moses. On a deeper level, however, Jewish believers demanded Gentile compliance with the Law of Moses because, from their perspective, only in complying with the rigid dietary and purity regulations could one be part of the *holy* people, clean and acceptable to God. If the community of faith was going to be a unified community of faith, everyone in it needed to be pure. Otherwise table fellowship was not possible. From a traditional Jewish perspective, unity, especially as it was expressed in the intimacy of table fellowship, could only exist when all believers maintained the highest standards of ritual purity.

Paul, however, viewed the matter from a different perspective: instead of requiring non-Jews to live as Jews, the Jews should understand that one's relationship with God no longer had anything to do with the external considerations related to ritual purity. They could continue to observe whatever Jewish customs they preferred, including dietary and other ritual concerns, as long as they understood that those traditions were of no spiritual value—as far as affecting relationship with God. Jewish believers could continue to observe Jewish customs, but could not require Gentiles to observe them. And Jewish believers must grow to the point of being comfortable enjoying table fellowship with non-Jews. How long would such growth take?

If, as many British scholars suggest, the events Paul describes in Galatians 2 occurred before the Acts 15 conference (Staples 1962:Vol. 1 599-607), it is clear that it took time for Jewish believers to come around to Paul's thinking. In Galatians 2, James is portrayed (at least by association with those who came from Jerusalem) as one who is opposed to table fellowship with Gentiles (*ca.* 46). But by the time of the conference in Acts 15 (*ca.* 49), James is at a very different place in his thinking. He may not yet be comfortable practicing table fellowship with Gentiles, but he acknowledges the rightness of Paul's perspective. Even if James had not previously been opposed to table fellowship with Gentiles, many Jews obviously were. It appears that Peter, at that earlier date, was not completely comfortable with the practice, for while he was in Antioch he crumbled under pressure from Jews (who were associates of James) and who were opposed to table fellowship.[11]

While the exact chronology of events related to the Jerusalem conference may not be available and supportable,

---

[11] To suggest that Peter was fully convinced of the rightness of table fellowship with Gentiles *and was comfortable with the practice* during his visit to Antioch, yet that he succumbed to the pressure of the Jerusalem Jews, is to suggest that he was more concerned about the opinion of the traditionalists than he was with what was right. It seems less offensive to suggest that Peter was not completely comfortable with the idea of Jew-Gentile table fellowship and succumbed to pressure, than to say that he was fully comfortable and simply disassociated himself from Gentile believers. Peter should be given the benefit of the doubt. Even if he had been intellectually and theologically convinced, given his experience at Cornelius' home, intellectual ascent and emotional comfort are two very different things.

the underlying issues that incited the events are clear. And while the issue of table fellowship may not be directly mentioned in Acts 15, it is clearly a related issue (Esler 1987:98). Given the prohibitions the Jewish believers asked the Gentile believers to observe, this seems clear. The letter the Jerusalem leaders wrote to the Gentile believers asked them to avoid four things: 1) eating food offered to idols, 2) consuming blood, 3) eating the meat of strangled animals, and 4) sexual immorality. Three of the prohibitions have to do with food, one has to do with sexual relations. Even when writing to say that non-Jewish believers did not need to comply with the Law of Moses, Jewish believers could not seem to refrain from suggesting that Gentile believers pay attention to basic issues related to purity. While it is possible to discuss each of the four prohibitions outside the context of ritual purity (for instance, avoiding eating meat sacrificed to an idol can be discussed strictly in the context of avoiding idolatry), can it really be denied that basic purity concerns, as they were understood by the Jerusalem Jews, provide the foundation for the prohibitions?

By this point in his Acts narrative, Luke has demonstrated that bringing Gentiles into the community of faith was God's doing, and that the church leaders have accepted the idea and made provision for interaction between the two groups of believers. The four remaining table fellowship texts in Luke's narrative demonstrate that Jew-Gentile table fellowship is entirely acceptable—an idea with which many of Luke's readers may have been struggling.

Acts 16:11-15, 40

Readers not familiar with the table fellowship controversy could read this (and the following three texts) without ever seeing what Luke's Jewish readers would have seen immediately: Paul and his Jewish mission team accepting the hospitality (which included table fellowship) of not only a Gentile, but a Gentile *woman.*

Luke's inclusion of this material is no accident or casual mentioning of an insignificant detail. Part of his plan has been to demonstrate not only that complete, unrestricted table fellowship in the community of faith is acceptable, but that it is *essential* to completing the task Jesus gave his followers. Jesus told his followers that when they went out preaching they were not to worry about what kind of food they were given to eat. They could not travel the world preaching the gospel if they were constantly worried about ritual dietary concerns. Luke recorded Jesus' instructions regarding those matters, and now he is demonstrating on a very practical level how those instructions are to be carried out.

It is interesting that immediately after Luke's recording of the events in Jerusalem concerning Gentiles and the law (chapter 15), which were directly related to the issue of table fellowship, Luke begins to illustrate the point by showing Paul and his mission team interacting closely with Gentiles without regard to purity issues (chapter 16).

Heil notices that Lydia "urged" Paul and his team to stay with her. He concludes from this that since the word translated urge (*parabiazomai*) can mean "prevail upon" or "force" that Paul and his mission team did not want to stay with her (presumably because she was a Gentile) but that she pushed the issue until they had to comply (1999:275-276). Heil's conclusion is unwarranted. While the word can mean to prevail upon, carrying the idea of insisting to the point of leaving the person no choice, such an understanding of the word is not necessary. It can simply mean to urge, as in, *Please stay at my home. I would feel terrible if you had to stay somewhere else. Please accept my hospitality.* There is no reason to believe that Paul, the champion of Jew-Gentile equality, had a problem enjoying table fellowship with a Gentile. If there was a concern in his mind at all, it was more likely related to the propriety of four men (Paul, Silas, Timothy and Luke) being hosted by a single woman.

Acts 16:30-34

While Paul and his mission team were enjoying Lydia's hospitality in the city of Philippi, their work resulted in Paul and Silas being arrested, beaten, and jailed. After the miraculous events that resulted in Paul assuring the distraught jailer that there was no need to harm himself, the jailer asked what to do to be saved. Paul told him. He and Silas were then taken out of the jail, treated kindly, and were eventually taken to the jailer's home. There was more preaching and the jailer's entire household believed and were baptized. Paul and Silas were served a meal. No questions were asked regarding what kind of food they were being served or how it had been prepared. Paul and Silas followed Jesus' instructions and simply ate what they were given.

This is a significant text in Luke's narrative because it adds another dimension to his ongoing presentation of table fellowship across social and cultural boundaries. Unlike Cornelius and Lydia, the jailer was not already a God-fearer. He was simply a pagan. Yet Paul and Silas had no problem going to his home and eating with him. Luke's Jewish readers would have been challenged and stretched as they read his account of the expansion of the community of faith.

Acts 18:7-8

This is another text where contemporary readers may completely miss the subtle yet highly significant information provided by Luke regarding Jew-Gentile table fellowship. Not long after arriving in Corinth, Paul found himself at odds with unbelieving Jews in the synagogue. If they were not interested in his good news he would go to the Gentiles.

However, Paul not only preached to the Gentiles, he accepted an offer of hospitality from Titus Justice, a Gentile God-worshipper, staying in his home while continuing his work in Corinth. Paul worked in Corinth for approximately eighteen months. Presumably he enjoyed Titus' hospitality and table fellowship the entire time.

While this brief mention may escape our notice, it is unlikely that it escaped the notice of Luke's original readers, especially Jewish readers. How could a Jew live in a Gentile home for a year and a half and not be contaminated, becoming ritually impure? He could not. The only thing that could make table fellowship between Jews and Gentiles possible was in setting aside the traditions regarding ritual purity.

Acts 27:33-34

Again, the significance of this event would have been remarkable for Luke's Jewish readers. Here was a Jew, one who approached Judaism from the Pharisaic tradition, acting as the host for a group of pagan sailors in a shipboard meal. It is highly unlikely that the bread Paul broke could have been ritually acceptable—proper ingredients properly prepared. Yet he not only ate it, he ate it along with the non-Jewish crew and passengers of the ship.

Why would Luke include four incidents of unrestricted Jew-Gentile table fellowship in his narrative after his lengthy accounts of Cornelius' conversion and the Jerusalem conference if he was not specifically demonstrating how those events impacted believers who were charged with the responsibility of proclaiming the good news to all the nations?

Summary of Table Fellowship in Acts

Initial accounts of table fellowship in Acts occur between members of the community of faith in Jerusalem (Ac. 2:41-47). However, it must be remembered that in such a large crowd there would have been Jews who did not place as much emphasis on ritual purity as did others. Thus, Luke begins immediately to hint that ritual purity was not an immense concern.

However, old ways die hard. It was not long before a problem arose that was related to table fellowship concerns. The Hellenistic Jewish widows were being discriminated against in the daily distribution of food (Ac. 6:1-7). Why? Because they were Hellenistic rather than Palestinian. What difference did that make? Most likely, the Hellenistic believers were perceived by the Palestinian believers to be less concerned about matters related to purity. Palestinian believers, especially those who were Pharisees, did not appreciate or encourage contact with them.

The first difficulty in the church arose over matters related to purity issues. The apostles dealt with the matter effectively, but in telling the story, Luke illuminates for us the difficulties involved. If issues of purity were significant between Jews of different sociocultural backgrounds, how significant were they going to be between Jews and Gentiles? Yet did not Jesus command his followers to disciple all ethnic groups?

The events that occurred at Cornelius' home (Ac. 10:1-11:18) were monumental in scope, impacting the community of faith in ways those early believers could not have imagined. The sociocultural boundaries that had been crossed to that point were utterly insignificant compared to what Peter did when he entered Cornelius' home and ate with him. In recording these events, Luke was not only demonstrating what had happened, but what *must* happen if

113

Jesus' command to proclaim the good news to all nations was to be obeyed.

In addition to the events at Cornelius' home, the debates concerning Gentiles and the Law of Moses (which were really about ritual purity), and the subsequent conference in Jerusalem (Ac. 15) were also highly significant for the community of faith. They led to an *official* policy formulated and articulated by the church leaders regarding Gentiles and their responsibilities concerning Jewish law and customs.

Luke is careful to note that the church leaders believed that the Holy Spirit was working with them in their decision and preparation of the document outlining their position. Thus, their decision was also God's decision—a decision that did not require non-Jewish believers to observe traditions related to ritual purity. For some Jewish believers, such a decision was nearly incomprehensible. How could anyone be part of the holy people of God and not observe the purity rituals that made one holy? They were being asked to re-think the foundational assumptions of their theology.

To assist his readers in this re-evaluation of their theological assumptions, Luke not only reports the events and decisions that will bring Jews and Gentiles together in unrestricted table fellowship, he utilizes four texts (Ac. 16:11-15, 40; 16:30-34; 18:7-8; 27:33-34) to demonstrate for his readers that Jewish believers are, in fact, enjoying unrestricted social interaction and table fellowship with Gentiles.

Luke has not lectured his readers regarding table fellowship. He has demonstrated what God has done among his people and how leaders in the community of faith, those working among Jews and those out working in the Gentile world, have handled the issues. Luke has made it clear that God expects his people to cross social and cultural boundaries in obedience to Jesus' command to preach the Gospel to all nations.

114

Contemporary Missiological Implications
of Table Fellowship in Luke-Acts

We have considered the implications of Luke's handling of table fellowship concerns in relation to the first century community of faith. What are the missiological implications of those issues for the community of faith today?

Table Fellowship Beyond the Table

Table fellowship was not just about eating. What one ate was important, to be sure. But so were the people with whom one ate. Why? Because it implied a sameness, a connection, a shared perspective on an array of important issues, an equality, an intimacy that bound people together. The sociocultural barriers that divided people melted away when people sat down to enjoy a meal together. Eating together implied a level of fellowship and community that God knew his people would need to enjoy if they were to participate with each other and with him in accomplishing his purpose in the world. Of course, such intimacy was not possible if ritual purity (rooted primarily in dietary regulations) stood as a barrier between people of different cultures.

Luke was concerned about table fellowship because God was concerned about table fellowship. It is not that God is concerned with what we eat. He is concerned with the level of relationship we enjoy with one another. He is concerned with our willingness to extend to others who are not like us an invitation to join us in relationship with God. God is concerned about our willingness to be open to people who live in social or cultural contexts that differ from our own. God is concerned with our willingness to cross the social and cultural barriers that separate us from others. Are we willing to cross those barriers, reaching out to those who

115

do not yet enjoy a relationship with God? Are we willing to enter into a *table fellowship kind* of relationship with them, enjoying a relationship with them that reflects the unity and intimacy God envisions for his people?

A *table fellowship kind* of relationship is what God wants his people to experience among themselves and to offer to others not yet part of the community of faith: a relationship expressed in terms of kindness and generosity of spirit, egalitarian interdependency, humility, commitment and sacrifice. We experience little hesitation enjoying such a relationship with those who have socioeconomic, sociopolitical, and sociocultural perspectives similar to our own. We are comfortable being with other people who are like us. But how comfortable are we, how willing are we to share the intimacies of table fellowship—and all that goes with it—with people who do not share our economic, political, or cultural perspectives? How real is our egalitarian interdependency when the person sitting across the table from us is racially different from us? How deep is our kindness and generosity of spirit when the person across the table from us represents a cultural perspective that we perceive to be hostile to our own? How real is our humility, commitment, and sacrifice when the person sitting across from us is poor, socially isolated, uneducated, unsophisticated, perhaps even dirty and uncouth or ill mannered? How willing are we to cross the boundaries (society's and our own) to make real, significant contact with people who are not like us—with people who are culturally or ethnically "other?"

Incarnational, Relational Social Intimacy—Living as the Family of God

God created human beings for relationship— relationship with each other and with him. Being God's holy people includes living in relationship with him and with our human brothers and sisters. Luke addressed the issue of social intimacy in terms of table fellowship. It is a metaphor which still resonates in our world today. If the church is to be God's people in the world in any real and meaningful sense the barriers that divide people must be torn down, the table must be set and the food must be served. Who better to do that than God's people? *"All things are ready, come to the feast."* I can remember singing those words when I was just a child. What will it take for those words to have meaning today?

Table fellowship does not seem to be a problem for foreign, cross-cultural missionaries. They live and work in cross-cultural contexts all over the planet. They are where they are precisely because they are not afraid or unwilling to cross social and cultural boundaries. Table fellowship and all that goes with it is not usually a problem "over there." It is a problem right here at home. The church in our contemporary multiethnic, pluralistic American society is failing to span the gulf between peoples. A few noble efforts at bridging the gulf in a meaningful way are bearing fruit. Thank God for his grace. But for the most part the church in America is not keeping pace with the dramatic increases in population among the various people groups represented in our multiethnic society.[12] Why not? Fear may be one

---

[12] According to the American Religious Identification Survey, conducted in 2001 by Barry Kosmin and Egon Mayer in conjunction with the Graduate Center of the City University of New York, racial breakdowns in all Christian churches in America are as follows: White 70%, Black 10%, Asian 3%, Hispanic 12%, All Others 5%. Compare those numbers to the percentage breakdowns of the general population: White 75.1%, Black 12.3%, Asian 3.6%, Hispanic 12.5%, Other 5.5%. Church population is an eerie reflection of the nation's general population. The question is, as minority population percentages increase in the general population, are there comparable increases in the percentages of minority population within the church? Is the church effectively reaching out across social and cultural boundaries to evangelize minority populations as those populations increase in society? Statistics which would provide

117

reason. We are often suspicious of things and people that are unfamiliar to us. Cultures that are unfamiliar to us naturally arouse suspicion. They make us uncomfortable. People from other cultures look different, sound different, and act different. Often there are too many differences for us to be comfortable interacting with them.

Another reason we don't interact well with people of other cultures may be our own standards of what is acceptable and unacceptable. Just as the Jews of the first century, we have our own social maps that guide us in our daily lives. These social maps suggest not only what may or may not be done, but when, where, how, and with whom. It is the *with whom* part that can inhibit our interaction with others. The *with whom* part of our social maps usually excludes interaction with people who are not part of our social group. Of course, we must remember that these social maps are not absolute in any sense. They are cultural guidelines that suggest behavior. However, people control the social maps. Social maps do not control people. We are free to ignore the *with whom* part of our social maps whenever we please.

What, then, must Christians do to in order to truly live as the family of God, enjoying table fellowship (and all that goes with it) with the amazing variety of people that make up American society? We must practice incarnational, relational social intimacy.

The concept of incarnational, relational ministry in a missions context is not a new idea. Missionaries have engaged in incarnational cross-cultural ministry for years. What about local ministry in a North American context? The idea of incarnational cross-cultural ministry in a North American context is not as familiar. This needs to change. We no longer live in a monocultural society. The people

---

an answer to this question do not seem to be available. My suspicion, however, is that we are not keeping up.

who live around us enjoy a different cultural heritage than we do. We must begin to think about local ministry as multiethnic ministry. Western ministers (pastors, preachers—whatever we want to call ourselves) must become Western missionaries, utilizing an incarnational approach in multiethnic ministry. Jesus, by means of incarnation, entered our world. He became one of us. He spoke a human language, ate human food, wore human clothes, suffered all the frailties of human existence. He identified himself with us. His becoming human was the way he accomplished his ministry mission.

In the same way, if we are to accomplish our ministry mission we must become one of the people we intend to serve. Our ministry must be *incarnational*, which means that it will be *relational*, which brings us back to the topic of table fellowship and the *social intimacy* that occurs when people sit down and enjoy a meal together.

The real key, however, for successful outreach across social and cultural boundaries in incarnational, relational ministry is to expand the effort to include not only church leaders, but members as well. It is essential that the church as a whole be mobilized. The simplest way to reach the lost is to touch the lost, to sit down with them and enjoy their company, to eat together, to experience life together, to let them see for themselves how our relationship with God makes a difference in our lives. This is incarnational ministry.

The church needs to be reminded that God invented culture, that he loves all the beautiful variation that exists in his world, including all the cultural variation that exists among his human children. If God appreciates and values cultural variation, we must learn to appreciate and value it as well.

How can we get the church to cross the social and cultural boundaries that exist in our society today? *First*, we need to pray about it. We need to ask God to motivate us to action. On the day of Pentecost flames of fire hovered above the disciples, signifying the Spirit's presence. Perhaps the church today needs God to light a fire under us, to motivate us to action.

Second, leaders must model the behavior they hope to see in the members who follow them. Leaders must be actively engaged in cross-cultural ministry, utilizing table fellowship as part of an incarnational, relational ministry.

Third, preaching and teaching in local churches must focus on the use of table fellowship as an appropriate and effective tool for cross-social and cross-cultural outreach. What better way to accomplish that than to utilize Luke-Acts in the pulpit and in the Bible class, focusing on Luke's account of table fellowship in Jesus' ministry and in the ongoing ministry of the early church?

Fourth, church leaders must assist members in cross-social and cross-cultural ministry by providing opportunities for contact and interaction with people of a local community. A little investigation into the needs of people in the community combined with a little creative thinking may result in a number of ways to bring people of the community in contact with church members so that social interaction and relationship building (table fellowship) is possible. If we will step out in faith God will bless our efforts. When the church as a whole begins to live as the family of God, inviting people to experience God in the fellowship of the community of faith, lives will be changed.

Spiritual events of amazing proportion can be set in motion by simply inviting someone to share a meal with you. Luke understood this. He presented the concept to his readers so they could see and experience the power of table fellowship.

Summary

Luke had a number of goals in mind as he wrote his two-volume narrative. There were several themes he wanted his readers to think about, to struggle with. One of those themes was table fellowship across social and cultural boundaries. To challenge his readers' assumptions about appropriate companionship during table fellowship, Luke's gospel presents Jesus engaging in table fellowship with people who were not considered acceptable company, especially at meals. Luke also writes about Jesus telling his followers not to worry about dietary concerns as they travel about preaching the Good News. Luke's point seems to be that Jesus was not worried about dietary concerns and ritual purity. He did not want his followers to be worried about them either. Instead, Jesus wanted his followers to engage people, relate to them, share the Good News with them so people can be reconciled to God.

Luke continues his table fellowship theme in Acts. The disciples are seen enjoying a family-like intimacy in the community of faith as they eat together. Believers of different social strata mix freely enjoying one another's company, caring for one another's needs. Everything was fine until significant cultural boundaries were crossed and traditions that had always safeguarded ritual purity were challenged and threatened. Luke's narrative includes those threats and the church's response to them in order to demonstrate to his readers that it is God's intention that cultural barriers be broken down so that the love of Christ can flow freely from culture to culture, from one people to another people.

The lesson for the church today is that table fellowship is just as important for effective outreach today as it was 2000 years ago. Our multicultural American society is a vast grid of intersecting lines, marking boundaries between social strata and cultural communities. Crossing those boundaries is essential. Tearing them down is even more essential. Table fellowship is one of the best ways to tear them down.

CHAPTER 4

DISCIPLESHIP IN LUKE-ACTS: ON THE WAY WITH JESUS AS PARTICIPANTS IN GOD'S MISSION

Luke has quite a bit to say about discipleship. It is one of the recurring themes of his two-volume work. Some basic considerations about discipleship need to be discussed, however, before moving on to the specifics of Luke's material.

Discipleship

Generally speaking, disciples were those people in the New Testament who enjoyed a special and intense relationship with Jesus (Weder 1992:Vol. 2, 207). Two Greek words are crucial to the study of discipleship: 1) *akoloutheo*, which means to go behind, to follow, metaphorically, as a pupil is a follower of his or her teacher (Blendinger 1975:Vol. 1, 480-483), 2) *mathetes*, a pupil, learner, apprentice, someone who is bound to someone in order to acquire his practical and theoretical knowledge (Müller 1975:Vol. 1, 483-490).
Michael Wilkins observes that:

> Discipleship can be narrowly understood in terms of the historical master-disciple relationship. . . It can also be understood more broadly as Christian experience, and what that way of life entails. To understand fully the Gospel portrait of discipleship, one must keep in view (1) the moment within the ministry of Jesus in which the challenge of discipleship is given to and lived out by the disciples, (2) the moment within the church's life when the would-be disciple is tested (1992:182)

Luke presents discipleship from both of these perspectives.

It is interesting to note that of the 261 times the word disciple or disciples (*mathetes*) occurs in the New Testament it is found in the Gospels or in Acts. Of the 92 times follow or follower (*akoloutheo*) occurs, 73 of them are in the Gospels or Acts. Clearly, following Jesus as one of his disciples was a foundational theme for all the Gospel writers. Since, Luke also wrote Acts, he is able to expand on the subject in a way Matthew, Mark and John cannot.

Discipleship Texts in Luke

The focus in this section will be on the details of each "discipleship" encounter Luke records.

Luke 5:1-11

This encounter at the Sea of Galilee has to do with the call of Peter, James and John. John makes it clear in his Gospel that this was not their first encounter with Jesus (Jn. 1:35-51). They had previously heard him teach and perhaps witnessed miracles he performed. Their interaction with him had not been merely as observers in a crowd. They had interacted with him on a personal level. Now Jesus is asking them to make a decision, a commitment concerning him. While Luke does not record the specific call or invitation to "follow me," as does Mark and Matthew, it seems clear from

Luke's account that Jesus did extend an invitation to them because: 1) at their distress over the large catch of fish (and their subsequent realization of the kind of person he was) Jesus calmed them, explaining that in the future they would "fishing" for people, and 2) they decided to leave their fishing business and become followers of Jesus.

In this text, those called to be Jesus' followers: 1) witnessed his supernatural power, 2) were informed of the missionary nature of Jesus' ministry and the training they would receive in that regard, 3) left their business, and 4) followed Jesus as his disciples.

Luke 5:27-32

The call of Levi is both similar and dissimilar to the call of Peter, James and John. A key difference is that Luke does not record Levi being witness to Jesus' supernatural power. However, Luke's failure to record such an event does not mean that the event did not occur. In fact, to suppose that Levi was fully aware of who Jesus was, what he taught and the supernatural power at his disposal lends credibility to Levi's willingness to leave a lucrative form of income to become a disciple of Jesus. Why would one become a disciple (an apprentice) of anyone without knowing what was involved? What would he be learning? What kind of work would he be doing? It is likely that like Peter, James, and John, Levi knew who Jesus was before Jesus called him into apprenticeship. Jesus knew who Levi was and called him to discipleship based on his suitability for the mission Jesus had in mind.

As Peter, James and John left everything to follow Jesus, so, too, Levi left his tax business[13] to become a follower of

---

[13] While Levi is referred to as a tax collector, Zacchaeus is referred to as a chief tax collector. Zacchaeus was most likely a tax "farmer" buying from the Roman government something similar to a franchise license, giving him the right to collect taxes in a given geographic region. He

Jesus. Levi understood that if he was going to follow Jesus there would have to be changes in his circumstances. Following required leaving—forsaking.

Another similarity between the call of the previous disciples and that of Levi is the missionary aspect of discipleship. It is certainly possible to view Levi's banquet as a celebration of his new status as a follower of Jesus. However, it may be more in keeping with the ministry context of Jesus and the call to a *missionary-oriented* discipleship to view the banquet as an opportunity to introduce his friends to Jesus, that is, to view the banquet as an opportunity for evangelistic outreach.

Another feature of this discipleship text is that Jesus associates with people who are considered unacceptable company. In attending a dinner with tax collectors and other *sinful* people, Jesus crossed social boundaries that people who considered themselves *righteous* were unwilling to cross. Jesus, however, was willing to enjoy table fellowship with people normally considered unacceptable company.

In this text, then, we see discipleship involving: 1) an invitation to follow Jesus, 2) an accepting of that invitation, which involved a leaving of the old way of life to begin a new way of life, 3) missionary outreach that, 4) crossed social boundaries and included table fellowship.

Luke 6:12-16

Though this text has to do with Jesus appointing twelve of his disciples to be apostles, it is very much a part of Luke's presentation of discipleship in his two-volume

---

then would have employed men like Levi to do the actual collecting at tax booths or "offices" at various locations. A tax farmer, like Zacchaeus, would have been much wealthier than a tax collector like Levi. However, both of them would have been disliked by their fellow citizens for aligning themselves with Rome for financial gain (Bamberger 1962:Vol. 4, 522).

narrative. After a night in prayer, Jesus selected twelve of his followers to be specially trained and designated as future leaders of his movement. A number of factors are crucial: 1) the selection of those who would be the leaders of the disciples came from among the disciples, 2) the selection came only after much prayerful consideration, 3) the fact that they were called "apostles" continues to imply the missionary nature of discipleship, for the word means *delegate, messenger, one sent forth with orders.* Of course, the orders they were eventually given and the message they were sent to deliver had to do with the Good News they were to preach to all the nations (24:44-47).

In this text it becomes clear that 1) there must be leaders even among followers, 2) that (as far as Jesus was concerned) leaders (who were also still followers) should be appointed from among the followers, and 3) appointing leaders is serious and should only be done after a great deal of serious prayer and reflection.

Luke 10:1-20

There is a tendency to think of Jesus' disciples as a small group, perhaps the apostles and just a few others. This text however, reminds us that for much of Jesus' ministry he had a substantial group of disciples. In this text, Luke records Jesus' selection and sending out of seventy-two of them on a preaching tour. The twelve were probably included in the seventy-two. Their mission was to go ahead of Jesus to the towns and villages he would visit on his way to Jerusalem, preparing them for Jesus' visit.

That the theme of this preaching tour was evangelistic (missionary oriented) is made clear by Jesus' use of the harvest metaphor. The disciples are to ask God to send more workers into the field to bring in the harvest of souls.

Jesus' instructions to his disciples as he sent them out are crucial to Luke's presentation of discipleship. Jesus tells them to: 1) go, 2) realize the dangers involved, 3) depend on God for what they need, 4) be a blessing to those they encounter, 5) not worry about ritual dietary regulations, 6) remember that those who reject the message are rejecting the Son and the Father.

What does this text tell us about discipleship? It tells us that discipleship: 1) is active—it involves going, 2) involves hardship—there can be danger from opposition, 3) involves being a blessing in the lives of others, 4) involves change, new directions, new priorities, 5) has little to do with external traditions and everything to do with internal truths, 6) includes preaching, or delivering a message, 7) involves rejection, and 8) involves the ultimate defeat of Satan.

Luke 18:18-30

This text, one of the better known Lucan texts, is central to Luke's discipleship theme. The rich man, a religious leader, asked Jesus how to attain eternal life. Jesus' response was essentially that the man already knew how to attain eternal life—live as God had directed him to live. The man said he had done that. Jesus did not dispute the man's claims. He simply added that there was one more thing the man needed to do: sell his possessions, give the proceeds to the poor and become a follower of Jesus. Of course, the man was saddened at the prospect of selling all he had and donating the proceeds to the poor, for he had a lot.

As the man walked away, Jesus commented to his disciples how hard it was for wealthy people to enter the Kingdom of God, that is, to give themselves fully to God. It was easier for a camel to go through the eye of a needle. This was especially difficult for the disciples to understand. According to their worldview, wealthy people were wealthy because God had blessed them. If wealthy people, who were thought to be especially favored and blessed by God (Geldenhuys 1951:460), had difficulty getting into the kingdom, what hope was there for the poor? It is somewhat ironic that the point Jesus was making was exactly opposite of the typical view of the people of that day. Without attempting to correct the erroneous assumptions of his followers, Jesus simply explained that since salvation ultimately depends on God, even the most difficult salvation cases can be handled by God. Peter, like an eager child seeking parental approval, points out that he and his fellow disciples had left all they had to follow Jesus. Jesus agreed, and assured Peter that anyone who sacrificed for God would be amply rewarded.

Two important questions come to mind when analyzing this text from a discipleship perspective: 1) why did Jesus tell the rich man to sell all he had and become a disciple, and 2) is such behavior expected of all disciples (Pilgrim 1981:89)? David Seccombe provides an overview of positions scholars have taken over the years in their attempts to explain why Jesus asked the rich man to sell his possessions and become a follower. One suggestion scholars have made is that the man's comment that he had observed or kept all the commandments was rooted in ignorance and misunderstanding. Jesus' goal, they suggest, was to demonstrate to the man that he had not been all that compliant. Seccombe rejects this suggestion, noticing that there is nothing in what Jesus says to warrant such a conclusion. Jesus accepts the man's claim of obedience without any kind of negative response.

Another suggestion as to why Jesus wanted the man to sell his possessions is that while he had kept the commandments he had not proactively gone out of his way to help the needy. Therefore, Jesus wanted him to be selfless and sacrificial in helping others. Seccombe rejects this notion, observing that Jesus' command to sell everything was too extreme if teaching charity was his goal.

A third suggestion scholars have made regarding Jesus' command to sell everything is that Jesus is indicating that there was an additional requirement for entrance into heaven. Seccombe rejects this suggestion on the basis that such a conclusion is simply not supported by the first part of the story. Jesus did not present himself as a rabbi suggesting some new requirements for getting into heaven.

Seccombe's suggestion is that Jesus' demand that the man sell his possessions and become a disciple involved an action that transcended obedience to the commandments (1982:118-124). While his criticisms of other explanations of Jesus' demands on the rich man are acceptable, his own explanation of the text is not satisfying. At least, his comments are so brief they could easily be misunderstood.

I believe Jesus' response to the rich man was rooted in genuine admiration for the man's sincerity. Mark makes this clear in his version of the story 10:21. The man had been obeying the law. But he wanted something more than that. He wanted to be sure that he was doing that which God would appreciate and reward. Was there something beyond simply keeping the law that he could do? Yes, he could give himself fully and completely to God, selling all he owned, giving the proceeds to the poor, and travel with Jesus as a disciple. If, as a way of absolutely insuring his entrance into the kingdom, the man wanted to go beyond what God had asked of his people, complete self-sacrifice and absolute dependence on God would get him what he wanted. That, unfortunately, appears to have been more than he was willing to do.

Does this mean the man could not go to heaven without selling all he owned? No. It means that if he wanted the extra assurance he would have to go the extra distance (in this case "all the way"). Since he was unwilling, he was limited to the normal occurrence: keep the law to the best of his ability and accept God's grace on the day of judgment.

If this is a correct interpretation, why did Jesus comment that it was difficult for wealthy people to enter the kingdom of God? Because there is a sense in which all those who would be disciples of Jesus must turn away from wealth. Disciples of Jesus will not think of wealth in terms of security, accomplishment, or satisfaction. Discipleship requires a radical re-prioritizing of one's thinking, one's loyalties, one's values. Wealth itself is not a problem. The problem is the attitude one has toward wealth. How important is wealth? What role does wealth play in one's life? Wealth can be a tool used to God's glory to help other people, or it can become something to be trusted, cherished, and horded. Acquiring wealth can become one's priority in life, one's god. Jesus understood that most people who have wealth tend to place a lot of trust in it. He understood how hard it is for wealthy people to control their wealth rather than allowing their wealth to control them. If a person has wealth, can he or she walk away from it if God asks him or her to do so? Most wealthy people cannot. That's what Jesus was talking about. Wealthy people have a hard time re-prioritizing their values so that money is not high on their list of important things. As long as money is of primary importance to a person, God cannot have the place in their lives he deserves.

This, then, brings us to the second question regarding discipleship and the story of the rich man: are all followers of Jesus required to sell their possessions and give the proceeds to the poor in order to be disciples? Obviously, Jesus' own apostles did not believe so. While Luke's presentation of the early church in Acts portrays a marvelous spirit of community and generosity among the believers (egs. 2:41-47, 4:32), it is clear that discipleship did not require the selling of all of one's possessions. Barnabas, for example, sold a field and brought the money to the apostles to be used for needy believers. But there is nothing in Luke's account to suggest that Barnabas sold everything. Indeed, the unfortunate incident with Ananias and Sapphira illustrates this point even better than Barnabas. Peter makes it clear that Ananias had the right to sell or not sell his property, and if he chose to sell it, he retained the right to decide what to do with the proceeds from the sale (Ac. 5:4). Clearly, discipleship in the early church did not require the selling of one's property.

This brings us back to Wilkins' point: that discipleship must be understood in both the narrow and the broad sense. During Jesus' earthly ministry, being a disciple of Jesus meant leaving one's former life behind and literally following Jesus. Afterward, being a disciple of Jesus meant following the teachings of Jesus, living a life of loving service to others. Such a life could be lived without forsaking all possessions, as long as one was willing to re-prioritize one's life and values, putting God ahead of every one else and every thing else—including money.

What, then, is Luke telling his readers about discipleship? He is suggesting that 1) it requires a radical re-prioritizing of one's values, and 2) that for some people the price of discipleship is too high.

Luke 24:44-49

Given the missionary focus of the discipleship texts in Luke, this text is foundational to understanding discipleship in Luke's narrative. At the home of Zacchaeus, Jesus had declared that he had come to seek and save the lost (Lk. 19:10). His purpose was mission—the reconciliation of all people. Because of the very nature of discipleship, Jesus' followers were also about mission, about the reconciliation of the lost. Thus, when Luke records the commissioning of Jesus' followers in this text, he is recording a pivotal event. Jesus has led the way. He has accomplished his goal, making it possible for all people to be reconciled to God. He has called people to follow him and has taught them how to fish for people, how to find and recover the lost sheep, how to make disciples. Now he sends them out to do what he has been training them to do.

The specifics of this text are interesting. First, Jesus re-interprets the Hebrew Scriptures for them so they can see how he, as God's promised messiah, has fulfilled them. Second, Jesus sends them out with the message of repentance and forgiveness of sins. Third, by telling them that they will be his witnesses, he is reminding them of the amazing things they have seen and experienced. Fourth, he tells them to wait (not to go out) until they have been empowered by the Holy Spirit. Then they will be ready to undertake the task he has assigned them.

What is Luke teaching his readers about discipleship in this text? He is suggesting that discipleship involves: 1) explaining (and perhaps re-interpreting) the Scriptures so people can understand what God has said, 2) telling a story designed to generate a response from those who hear— repentance, which results in their being forgiven of their sins, 3) witnessing to what one has experienced in his or her relationship with Jesus, 4) being empowered by the Holy Spirit to do what Jesus asks all his followers to do.

Summary of Discipleship Texts in Luke

From Luke's presentation of discipleship in his Gospel, discipleship (at least during Jesus' earthly ministry) involved or was in some way related to: 1) the witness of supernatural power, 2) missionary outreach, 3) an invitation to follow Jesus, 4) accepting or rejecting the invitation, 5) forsaking one's old way of life in order to accept Jesus' invitation to follow him, 6) following Jesus wherever he goes—even across social boundary lines, 7) hardship, 8) being a blessing to others, 9) a radical re-prioritizing of one's direction, purpose, and values, 10) explaining or re-interpreting the Scriptures, 11) delivering a message

133

designed to elicit a response, 12) witnessing to what one has seen and experienced as a disciple of Jesus, 13) empowerment by the Holy Spirit.

Discipleship Texts in Acts

We now turn our attention to Luke's presentation of discipleship in the book of Acts. During Jesus' earthly ministry one could literally leave one's home and family to follow Jesus. Being a disciple of Jesus was a very literal reality at that time. How did the concept of discipleship change after Jesus ascended back to heaven? What did it mean to be a follower of Jesus when one could no longer literally follow him from place to place? Perhaps Luke will make that clear in his Acts narrative.

Acts 1:1-14

The opening of Luke's second volume includes a brief review of the events of Jesus' last days on earth and his final encounter with his followers. It is interesting that the *Introduction* to Acts is rooted in discipleship concerns. Jesus' followers had a job to do, but the Holy Spirit was coming to help them do it. They were to wait for him before beginning the task. When the Spirit arrived and empowered the disciples, they were to begin their work. Their method was to be *centrifugal*, beginning in Jerusalem and radiating out in all directions until the story has been told everywhere on earth.

Luke lists the apostles by name and notes that they were together continually, along with Mary and several other women, as well as Jesus' brothers. For those early believers, discipleship involved community. The women were right there with the men, an integral part of the community. Jesus' brothers, James and Jude, who had not previously believed in him, had become believers. For some, belief and discipleship comes slowly.

What do these opening verses imply regarding discipleship? Luke demonstrates that: 1) even though Jesus has ascended back into heaven, his followers are still his followers, 2) discipleship is rooted in missionary outreach, 3) discipleship involves a connection with the Holy Spirit as he empowers disciples to do what Jesus has asked them to do, 4) discipleship involves being together with other disciples, and 5) for some, discipleship comes slowly.

Acts 1:15-26

Those who had been Jesus' followers, and who now had additional insights into what God had done among them, became a community of faith who maintained contact with one another, meeting often for times of prayer. These were Jesus' disciples. They numbered 120.

Peter was of the opinion that the vacancy resulting from Judas' suicide needed to be filled. Perhaps he understood the symbolic representation between twelve apostles and the twelve tribes of Israel and felt the symbolism important enough to warrant the selection of a replacement. The qualifications for apostleship suggested by Peter required a personal knowledge and experience of Jesus for an extended period of time during his ministry. The use of a lottery system assumed that Jesus, who had been given all authority in heaven and on earth (Mt. 28:18), would select the individual he wanted to serve as one of his apostolic witnesses. Matthias was selected and became one of the twelve.

What has this event to do with discipleship in Luke-Acts? It provides further evidence that followers need leaders and that those leaders themselves must also be dedicated followers, appointed from among the disciples.

This event also demonstrates that those early believers understood that they were to carry on the mission and ministry Jesus had begun; and that discipleship was rooted in witnessing to Jesus' resurrection. This speaks volumes regarding the missionary nature of discipleship as those early believers understood it.

Luke, therefore, continues to focus on the 1) relationship between discipleship and community, 2) importance of leaders among the disciples, 3) the seriousness of the selection of leaders, and 4) the missionary nature of discipleship.

Acts 2:14-47

Six events stand as pivotal in the history of humankind: 1) the creation of human beings in God's image, 2) their fall into sin, 3) God becoming a human being in the person of Jesus, 4) his death on the cross, 5) his resurrection, and 6) the coming of the Holy Spirit on the day of Pentecost. The first two are beyond the scope of Luke's work. The incarnation, death and resurrection of Jesus, however, are key features of Luke's story. Having recoded those events in volume one of his two-part work, Luke turns his attention to the coming of the Holy Spirit.

God had foretold the outpouring of the Spirit (Joel 2:28-32). John the Baptist had said that Jesus would baptize people in the Holy Spirit (Lk. 3:16). Jesus had predicted the coming of the Spirit (Ac. 1:5, 8). All of these references are to the coming of the Holy Spirit on the day of Pentecost. The pouring out of the Spirit (from a heavenly point of view) is the same as the baptism of (or being baptized in) the Holy Spirit (from an earthly point of view). The Spirit was poured out into the world to be available and present in the lives of Jesus' followers in a way that he had not previously been available. Peter describes the presence of the Spirit in the

136

lives of believers as a gift, given to them when they are baptized (Ac. 2:38).

The Spirit begins immediately to empower Jesus' followers, enabling them to accomplish the task Jesus gave them. The Spirit generated a sound which drew a crowd. He then manifested his presence in flames of fire hovering over the believers, and by empowering them to speak in languages they had never learned. Peter steps forward to do the work he was called, trained and empowered to do, preaching about Jesus and salvation from sin.

The promise of forgiveness of sins and the gift of the Spirit is not only available to those present on that occasion, but also to the Gentiles, who are, at that moment, still *far away*. Those who believed Peter's message repented and were baptized, becoming part of the community of faith. They became disciples of Jesus. But in what sense? They could not literally follow Jesus. How, then, were they his disciples? Luke describes their behavior. They participated fully in the community of believers, devoting themselves to learning from the apostles, enjoying fellowship, communion, and regular prayer. They also shared their material possessions, an indication that they had adopted a new (and somewhat radical) view regarding wealth and possessions. They were, in every sense, followers of the Way, which meant they were followers of Jesus. Their discipleship was rooted in faith, but a faith that included personal experience through and with the indwelling Spirit. While their experience of Jesus may not have involved literally leaving their former lives behind to follow Jesus from place to place, they did, in a very real sense, leave their former lives behind and embrace a new way (Jesus' way) of experiencing and interpreting life. Their perspectives and values were reshaped. They were revitalized, reoriented, and redirected to a life centered in Jesus. If they followed Jesus' teachings, they followed Jesus.

What, then, does Luke show us regarding discipleship in the earliest days of the church of Jesus? Luke's picture of discipleship at the very beginning of the church includes: 1) the active presence of the Holy Spirit, empowering disciples to do the job Jesus asked them to do, 2) repentance and baptism, which result in the forgiveness of sins and the indwelling presence of the Holy Spirit, 3) inclusion in a community of believers, 4) an outward looking vision and anticipation of others being included in that community, 5) an attitude toward wealth and possessions which allows them to give generously to those in need, 6) an interest and participation in fellowship rooted in teaching/learning, social intimacy, and prayer.

Acts 3:12-4:4

The healing of the beggar created an opportunity for Peter to speak to the crowd about Jesus. His message was not only very much to the point, it was specifically contextualized to his audience. It was not a sermon that could have been preached to Samaritans or Gentiles. It was specifically targeted toward the people of Jerusalem, who, not long before had cried out for Jesus' blood. They had done it in ignorance, but they had done it. Peter is unapologetic in his accusation. As in his message on the day of Pentecost, the solution to the problem included turning *from* sin and *to* God to enjoy the spiritual refreshing God had made possible through sending his messiah.

The people of Jerusalem responded and many of them became believers—disciples of Jesus. The number of male believers grew to be about 5000. Adding in women and young people could have brought the total number of believers to somewhere between 15,000 and 20,000. There was a price to pay, however, for being such an active group. Peter and John were arrested and put in jail. Jesus had told his followers that they would suffer. Luke is illustrating the reality to which Jesus had referred.

What do we learn about discipleship from this text? We see that being a disciple means: 1) taking advantage of opportunities God provides for ministry and witness, 2) being willing to give that which one has to give, 3) allowing oneself to be used by the Holy Spirit to accomplish God's will, 4) telling people the truth—telling them what they need to hear, even if it is an unpleasant reality, 5) calling people to repentance, 6) expecting to suffer for your beliefs and your willingness to proclaim the truth, 7) knowing that when God's message is delivered people will respond and be reconciled to God.

Acts 4:8-12

After a night in jail, Peter and John were interrogated and threatened by the religious leaders. As Jesus had promised, Peter was filled with the Holy Spirit and empowered to speak effectively in his and John's defense. Peter made it clear that the religious leaders should not assume that he or John was the source of power by which the crippled man was healed. The power came from Jesus. The glory belongs to him alone. He is the one God raised from the dead, the one Scripture referred to as the cornerstone, the cornerstone rejected by the builders. Through him alone can people enjoy salvation from sin.

Jesus' disciples: 1) depend on the Holy Spirit for assistance, 2) acknowledge and glorify Jesus as the source of their power, 3) proclaim him as the only source and means of salvation from sin.

Acts 5:29-32

In another incident of opposition from the religious leaders, Peter and the rest of the apostles boldly declared that they would obey God rather than the orders of the council. Peter then declared what he knew to be true: that Jesus is the resurrected Lord, the Prince and Savior. He and the other apostles had witnessed events which demonstrated who Jesus really was. They witnessed to those events by the things they said. The Spirit added his "voice" to their testimony by the things he did—that is, the signs and wonders he enabled believers to perform.

In this text, discipleship involves: 1) loyalty and submissiveness to God before all others, 2) proclaiming what one knows to be true by virtue of experience, 3) a cooperative effort with the Holy Spirit to witness concerning Jesus.

Acts 9:1-19

Saul's call to discipleship was considerably different than the call of Peter, James and John. Saul was an aggressive opponent of those who believed Jesus to be God's messiah. Saul's call to discipleship is recorded three times in the book of Acts. In this text, Luke describes the events as the narrator of the text. In 22:6-16 and 26:12-18, Paul tells of his conversion as part of his legal defense to the crowd in Jerusalem and in Caesarea before King Agrippa. Each account is basically the same, with the account in 26:12-18 including some additional material.

Saul is confronted and blinded by Jesus, who asks Saul why he is persecuting him. The 26:12-18 account includes a comment from Jesus that it is hard for Saul to continue to kick against the goad. Bruce explains that the likely meaning of this comment is that Saul was already beginning to feel or believe that Jesus was indeed God's messiah, but that he was fighting the inclination to believe (1954:491). The goad or nudge to believe was there, but Saul was fighting it.

As Saul fought the inclination to believe, he was persecuting Jesus' followers. But Jesus said Saul was persecuting him. The implication is that if Saul was persecuting Jesus' followers, he is persecuting Jesus. Saul asked for the identity of the one speaking to him. Jesus complied, identifying himself simply as Jesus, then told Saul to go into the city and wait for instructions. Two further implications seem obvious: 1) Saul knew full well who Jesus was and knew who was speaking to him, and 2) Jesus knew that Saul was convinced, so that when the instructions were delivered he would obey.

In Paul's account of the story in 26:12-18, Jesus gave Saul additional instructions regarding his new mission and how God would use (and protect) him to accomplish his divine purpose.[14] Saul obeyed Jesus, going into the city and waiting to be contacted. Jesus then spoke to a disciple in Damascus named Ananias, telling him to go to Saul. Ananias knew who Saul was and did not want to go. Jesus, however, was firm and Ananias submitted and obeyed. Saul also obeyed when Ananias told him what to do. Saul was healed of his blindness and he was baptized, washing away his sins (22:16).

What lessons about discipleship does Luke provide us with in these texts about the conversion of Saul? Discipleship: 1) sometimes develops out of serious internal conflict, 2) sometimes develops in conjunction with a physical crisis, 3) involves a call to acknowledge Jesus as Lord, 4) requires obedience, 5) involves a new beginning—a symbolic washing, signaling the spiritual birth of a new child of God, 6) is missionary in nature, 7) involves hardship, and 8) requires trust in the Lord's protection.

---

[14] In this text, similar instructions (though not identical) were given to Saul by Ananias. Compare 9:15-16 with 26:16-17.

141

Acts 10:1-48

As Saul and Ananias in the previous text, both Peter and Cornelius provide lessons about discipleship in this lengthy text. Peter, a mature, experienced disciple, and Cornelius, a fresh, new follower of Jesus found common ground and brotherhood where before there had been none. How so?

Peter (along with the rest of Jesus' followers) had failed to take the story of Jesus to the ends of the earth. Even though Jesus had told them to, they could not bring themselves to cross the cultural boundaries that might result in their being ritually defiled. Approximately ten years had passed and nothing had been done to reach the Gentiles. That was unacceptable. Peter (and the Jewish community of faith) needed a jolt. At the home of Simon the Tanner, Peter got one.

The sheet came down and the Lord spoke—a direct command. *"Rise, Peter. Kill and eat."* And Peter said, *"No."* How could he do that? Because discipleship is voluntary. Fortunately, God was patient and the vision was repeated two more times. As Peter pondered its meaning, he received another jolt: Gentile men were looking for him. He was to go with them to the home of a Gentile man. Peter would obey, but he was apprehensive. He took additional Jewish disciples with him to server as witnesses to all that happened while at the home of a Gentile.

Cornelius received something of a jolt himself—an angel appeared to him with instructions about sending for Peter. A human being, not an angel, would proclaim God's message to Cornelius. When Peter arrived, that is what he did. And when Cornelius heard, he believed. The Holy Spirit manifested his presence and approval by empowering Cornelius and his household to speak in languages they had not learned, just as he had in Jerusalem on Pentecost. Cornelius and his household were baptized and the door of faith was then open to the Gentiles of the world. Afterward Peter and the other Jews with him accepted Cornelius' invitation to "stay" with him for several days—a stay which would have involved table fellowship.

This text teaches us a great deal about discipleship. Discipleship: 1) is a long and ongoing process—a journey, 2) at times requires that we be jolted out of our complacency, 3) allows us to retain our free will, 4) requires God's patience, 5) sometimes involves challenges that stretch us, making us uncomfortable, 6) opens new opportunities for social and cultural interaction, 7) involves a new experience of and relationship with the Holy Spirit.[15]

Acts 13:1-12

As noted in a previous chapter, the Holy Spirit assumed oversight of the early church's missionary outreach. In this text, he selects Barnabas and Saul as missionaries to lead the effort to preach the Gospel to the Gentiles. Barnabas and Saul were part of the leadership team of the church in Antioch. As the leaders worshipped and fasted, the Holy Spirit made his will known to them. After more prayer and fasting the church sent out Saul and Barnabas as the Spirit had instructed.

Just as the Spirit empowered disciples, he also led them. Given Luke's account of the Spirit specifically directing Paul's team on their second mission tour, it is

---

[15] This is not to say that the Holy Spirit will descend on everyone and enable them to speak in languages they have not learned as he did in Jerusalem and in Cornelius' home. The Spirit can manifest himself however he pleases. Obviously he does not always choose to manifest himself in the same way. All believers must be open to the presence and activity of the Spirit in their lives. There is no such thing as a Christian without the Holy Spirit. But Christians can limit his power in their lives until his presence is reduced to a mere fact. He is there, but he is not allowed to do anything. This is likely what Paul had in mind when he said not to *quench* the Spirit.

certainly valid to assume that he was leading the first tour as well. The island of Cyprus was one of the Spirit's initial targets. It is interesting that of all the stories Luke could have told, the one he chose as his "lead" story of the first missionary tour had to do with an encounter with evil. Apparently he had a point to make about Jesus' disciples encountering the same kind of opposition (spiritual evil) Jesus encountered. Just as Jesus successfully opposed the forces of evil, so his disciples, by the power of the Holy Spirit, can also oppose and defeat the forces of evil.[16] Paul's confrontation with evil resulted in positive results as the governor was impressed by what he observed. Opposing evil does not always require that supernatural power be applied in a physical way, as in blinding an opponent. When Jesus' disciples stand for the truth against the lies of Satan, they are confronting and opposing evil.

From this text Luke reminds us that discipleship: 1) involves a close working relationship with the Holy Spirit, 2) involves submission to the Spirit's will as he leads and guides, 3) is missionary in nature, 4) involves *going*— sometimes great distances, 5) involves confrontations with the forces of evil.

Acts 13:16-52

This lengthy text provides a glimpse into the missionary dynamics of discipleship. In Antioch of Pisidia Paul and Barnabas visit a local synagogue. They were given

---

[16] The forces of evil manifest themselves in many different ways. The Spirit can respond, and empower his people to respond, in many different ways as well. Striking someone blind may not be the way the Spirit chooses to oppose evil today. The Spirit may not empower disciples to do the same kinds of things he empowered them to do in the first century (though he certainly may), but he does still empower those who will let him empower them—those who want to work with him in opposing evil and calling people to repentance and reconciliation.

an opportunity to speak and Paul made good use of it. Paul's sermon, as Luke records it—which is probably a composite, overview, or summary of what Paul said (Johnson 1992:Vol. 4, 409)—is for the most part an overview of Israelite history, designed to lay the appropriate groundwork for the introduction of Jesus as the messiah of God. It is Jewish through and through and would be of little use to a non-Jewish audience. However, the sermon hit its mark and a number of Jews as well as God-fearers who worshiped in that synagogue asked Paul and Barnabas to return the following week. Over the course of the week, word spread throughout the city and the following Sabbath almost the entire city, Luke says, was present to hear Paul and Barnabas. Whether Luke means the entire Jewish population, the Jewish population plus God-fearers, or literally the whole population is unclear. Perhaps he simply meant that a large number of people were present. Either way, the Jewish leaders did not like the enthusiastically positive response Paul and Barnabas got. They spoke against them in an effort to discredit them.

The opposition of the Jewish leaders must have been considerable, for Paul's reaction (denouncing the Jews and turning to the Gentiles) would be inappropriate unless significant numbers of Jews responded negatively to his message about Jesus. The Gentiles were delighted. Many of them believed and the Gospel spread throughout the region. The Gospel stirs strong emotions. Unbelieving Jews so aggressively opposed Paul and Barnabas that they left the area. The new believers in Antioch, however, were not left to struggle on their own. They were filled with the Holy Spirit and with joy.

In this text, discipleship: 1) means taking advantage of the opportunities the Lord provides, 2) includes contextualizing the message to meet the sociocultural needs of the hearers, 3) means being prepared for a mixed response—positive and negative, and 4) includes realizing that sometimes the prudent thing to do is to move on to more fertile ground.

Acts 14:8-20

Paul and Barnabas' experience in Lystra provides an interesting lesson in discipleship, specifically as it relates to missions. The fact that Paul and Barnabas had been sent out by the Holy Spirit and that he worked closely with them did not mean that they were incapable of mistakes. I believe their unfortunate experience in Lystra was due to a miscalculation on their part—sadly, a miscalculation that many missionaries since then have repeated.

Paul and Barnabas' miscalculation was in assuming that their audience shared the same assumptions and perspectives that they did. Paul and Barnabas' normal plan of action was to go into the synagogue in each town. There they would encounter the Jews and God-fearing Gentiles, people they assumed would be most open to the message they had come to deliver. Normally this was the case. They almost always encountered some opposition, but also usually found a number of people, both Jews and Gentiles who eagerly embraced their message.

When Paul and Barnabas arrived in Lystra they may have followed the same procedure, going to the synagogue to preach—assuming there was a synagogue there. The problem in Lystra, however, occurred beyond the context of the synagogue, perhaps in a market place or some other outdoor setting. While preaching, Paul healed a lame man. The Lystrans, observing the miracle, supposed that they were being favored by a visit from the gods, which obligated them to honor their divine guests with a sacrifice. When Paul and Barnabas became aware that a sacrifice was to be offered to them they were shocked and horrified.

How could such a horrible misunderstanding have occurred? To place all the responsibility for the misunderstanding on the Lystrans is far too simplistic. Luke specifically notes that when the people responded to the miracle they observed, they cried out in their native dialect, which was Lyconian (Bruce 1954:290-291). Paul and Barnabas were mostly likely speaking Greek, the common trade language. Otherwise why would Luke have specified that the Lystrans cried out in their native dialect? It may have been that the Lystrans did not fully understand the message Paul and Barnabas proclaimed because of linguistic differences. Spiritual matters are best discussed and understood in one's "heart language.," rather than a secondary trade language—which is what Greek was to Lystrans. However, even if they understood completely what Paul and Barnabas were saying, they would have understood the message from their existing religious perspective. Local tradition held that Zeus and Hermes had assumed human forms and visited people in the area. When the people saw the miracle, they simply assumed the gods had come to visit them again, (Willimon 1988:126). Were Paul and Barnabas aware of this local lore? They should have been. Paul and Barnabas should have anticipated how the people might react to a miraculous healing.

Another factor in the misunderstanding may have been Paul's level of education. He was an educated man. Perhaps the Lystrans were not as educated or sophisticated as Paul imagined. Perhaps his presentation was a little beyond them. They would have understood part of the message, but somewhere along the way misunderstanding occurred—perhaps due to linguistic and cultural differences not understood or anticipated by Paul and Barnabas.

I believe Paul and Barnabas made three mistakes—mistakes still common to many missionary endeavors: 1) they assumed that the people to whom they were speaking would understand what was being said without any trouble, 2) Paul and Barnabas probably spoke the common trade language (Greek) rather than the local dialect, 3) they failed to take into account the influence of local religious traditions and perspectives. In other words, Paul and Barnabas failed to contextualize their message.

The Holy Spirit was working in, with, and through Paul and Barnabas. But that did not make them incapable of methodological error. Sometimes the best way to "teach" someone is to allow them to discover a reality on their own, to let them make mistakes and learn from them. I believe Paul learned how important it is to contextualize the gospel from his experience in Lystra. When Paul wrote to the Corinthians about becoming all things to all people, learning to think as they think, in order to save them (1 Cor. 9:20-23), he may have been reminded of his experience in Lystra.

The lessons related to discipleship in this text are that: 1) the Spirit does not control disciples to the point that mistakes are not possible, and 2) the process of growth and learning in the missionary enterprise is one of *action, reflection,* and *action,* that, is, accomplishing missionary activity, analyzing the effectiveness of what has been done, and making adjustments that allow for increased effectiveness, and then undertaking additional missionary activity.

Acts 15:1-31

By now the events of this chapter are familiar and rehearsing them in detail would be redundant. Reflection on the text from a discipleship perspective reveals a number of important insights. The disciples who were insisting that the Gentiles observe the Law of Moses were believers who, like Paul had a background in the *hasidim* movement, that is, the Pharisees, the pious ones (Martin 1975:Vol. 1, 84). There is no reason to assume that they were not conscientious, sincere believers who felt they were advocating proper behavior based on the truths of Scripture. They were, however, mistaken. Their mistake engendered debate, and, no doubt,

148

no small disturbance in the church. But disturbance or not, they were wrong and had to be stopped. Disciples who had been appointed leaders were called upon to evaluate, adjudicate and legislate in hopes of resolving the disagreement. They listened, they discussed, they responded. Was the problem solved? No. Not for a long time.

What do we learn about discipleship from this text? We learn that: 1) discipleship requires growth and change, 2) the growth and change do not necessarily come easily, and that not all disciples grow and change at the same rate, 3) in the process of ongoing discipleship disagreements and challenges will arise, 4) sometimes debate is necessary, 5) solutions and resolutions to problems seldom come easily or quickly.

Acts 17:16-34

From a discipleship/missiological perspective, the events of this text, which occurred in Athens, are best understood in contrast to the events that occurred in Lystra (14:8-20). There, Paul and Barnabas were somewhat inexperienced. Their inexperience resulted in an unfortunate misunderstanding. In this text, after many miles and several years of experience, Paul avoids similar mistakes. In his meanderings through the city, Paul reflects on the religious and spiritual implications of the things he sees. In observing the city and its people, Paul is getting to know them. He is learning what they value, how they live, how they communicate and interact. He is preparing to communicate with them in a way that minimizes the possibility of misunderstanding.

When an opportunity for a discussion with some Epicurean and Stoic philosophers presented itself, Paul took advantage. That discussion led him into another discussion with an influential group of thinkers. The discussion, as

Luke records it, does not include references to the Hebrew Scriptures or the "messiah." Instead, Paul referred to a local altar set up to "An Unknown God." This was Paul's starting point. From there he suggested that he knew this God who was, at that point, unknown to the Athenians. Paul's purpose was to introduce them to the God they did not know.

The story is quite familiar so they is no need to discuss it in detail. The point is that Paul contextualized his message. He knew God. His audience did not. Paul introduced and explained the one true God in a way that made sense to the people in their sociocultural context. There was no misunderstanding in Athens as there had been in Lystra. Perhaps there were several reasons why there was no misunderstanding. At least one of the reasons was that Paul contextualized his message better in Athens than he had in Lystra. There was disbelief in Athens, but not because they did not understand.

Lystra and Athens provide us with significant insights as to the importance of assumptions, language and religious paradigms. Paul was an educated man. So were the philosophers of Athens. Perhaps the people of Lystra were less sophisticated. Perhaps Paul did not take that into consideration as he spoke to them, assuming that they understood more than they did. We will never know for certain, but something in his presentation in Athens worked and something in his presentation in Lystra did not. To place all the blame for failed communication or all the credit for successful communication on the hearers and none on the speaker is not realistic. Paul shared his measure of both blame and credit in each communication context.

What lessons are there to be learned about discipleship from this text? In this text we see that discipleship: 1) involves times of reflection for the purpose of planning an effective contextualization strategy, 2) is rooted in missionary proclamation which will sometimes be well-received and sometimes not, 3) involves proclaiming a message that, even though it is contextualized, is essentially the same story told to all people so they can be reconciled to God.

Acts 20:17-38

In this text, Paul, a disciple, spoke to the leaders of the church in Ephesus. They, too, were disciples—shepherd-disciples, responsible for the spiritual development and well-being of the disciples under their care. Paul had "shepherded" these men. Now he encouraged them to pay close attention to their own shepherding responsibilities.

Paul's specific concern for the church in Ephesus had to do with the danger of false teachers—dangerous wolves among vulnerable sheep. The shepherds were to feed and protect the church. What did that mean? It meant they were to teach and assist the disciples in their spiritual development. It meant they were to pay attention to what was being taught. *Healthy teaching* was Paul's concern. Healthy teaching is that which results in healthy spiritual growth and maturity. Mature disciples lead the way, teaching, advising and living out their faith, providing an example for newer, less mature disciples to follow.

What does Luke teach us about discipleship in this text? Discipleship: 1) is an ongoing process of growth, 2) involves different levels of maturity and responsibility, 3) requires vigilance, 4) requires that the strong care for the weak, 5) involves struggle and sometimes danger, and 6) involves the sadness of separation as some disciples are called to make great sacrifices.

Summary of Discipleship Texts In Acts

We have examined fourteen passages in the book of Acts that provide us with glimpses into what it meant to be a disciple of Jesus in the first century after his earthly ministry had ended. This section will be a summary of those findings.

To be a follower of Jesus after his ascension back into heaven had a slightly different meaning than it did during his earthly ministry. During Jesus' earthly ministry, being his disciple, in its most literal sense, meant leaving one's home to follow him from place to place. However, after his ascension back into heaven, being his disciple precluded literally following him from place to place. What, then, did it mean? Obviously, there was a symbolic sense in which one was his follower, his apprentice, learning how to live as he had lived, to minister as he had ministered. As Luke's story unfolds in the book of Acts, what do we learn about discipleship?

Instead of making one very long list of the characteristics of discipleship found in Acts, it may be more helpful to present each of the fourteen summaries separately, noting again the characteristics or features of discipleship in Acts. It is interesting to note the recurring themes.

In Acts, Luke demonstrates that: 1) even though Jesus has ascended back into heaven, his followers are still his followers, 2) discipleship is rooted in missionary outreach, 3) discipleship involves a connection with the Holy Spirit as he empowers disciples to do what Jesus has asked them to do, 4) discipleship involves being together with other disciples, and 5) for some, true discipleship comes slowly.

Important elements of discipleship include: 1) the relationship between discipleship and community, 2) the importance of leaders among disciples, 3) the seriousness of the selection of leaders, and 4) the missionary nature of discipleship.

Luke's picture of discipleship at the very beginning of the church includes: 1) the active presence of the Holy Spirit, empowering disciples to do the job Jesus asked them to do, 2) repentance and baptism, which result in the forgiveness of sins and the indwelling presence of the Holy Spirit, 3) inclusion in a community of believers, 4) an outward looking vision and anticipation of others being included in the community of faith, 5) an attitude toward wealth and possessions which allows one to give generously to those in need, 6) an interest and participation in fellowship rooted in teaching/learning, social intimacy, and prayer.

Being a disciple means: 1) taking advantage of opportunities God provides for ministry and witness, 2) being willing to give that which one has to give, 3) allowing oneself to be used by the Holy Spirit to accomplish God's will, 4) telling people the truth—telling them what they need to hear, even if it is an unpleasant reality, 5) calling people to repentance, 6) expecting to suffer for your beliefs and your willingness to proclaim the truth, 7) knowing that when God's message is delivered people will respond and be reconciled to God.

Jesus' disciples: 1) depend on the Holy Spirit for assistance, 2) acknowledge and glorify Jesus as the source of their power, 3) proclaim him as the only source and means of salvation from sin.

Discipleship involves: 1) loyalty and submissiveness to God before all others, 2) proclaiming what one knows to be true by virtue of experience, 3) a cooperative effort with the Holy Spirit to witness concerning Jesus.

Discipleship: 1) sometimes develops out of serious internal conflict, 2) sometimes develops in conjunction with a physical crisis, 3) involves a call to acknowledge Jesus as Lord, 4) requires obedience, 5) involves a new beginning—a symbolic washing, signaling the spiritual birth of a new child of God, 6) is missionary in nature, 7) involves hardship, and 8) requires trust in the Lord's protection.

Discipleship: 1) is a long and ongoing process—a journey, 2) at times requires that we be jolted out of our complacency, 3) allows us to retain our free will, 4) requires God's patience, 5) sometimes involves challenges that stretch us, making us uncomfortable, 6) opens new opportunities for social and cultural interaction, 7) involves a new experience of and relationship with the Holy Spirit.

Discipleship: 1) involves a close working relationship with the Holy Spirit, 2) involves submission to the Spirit's will as he leads and guides, 3) is missionary in nature, 4) involves going—sometimes great distances, 5) involves confrontations with the forces of evil.

Discipleship: 1) means taking advantage of the opportunities the Lord provides, 2) includes contextualizing the message to meet the sociocultural needs of the hearers, 3) being prepared for a mixed response—positive and negative, and 4) realizing that sometimes the prudent thing to do is to move on to more fertile ground.

Of discipleship, it can be said that: 1) the Spirit does not control disciples to the point that mistakes are not possible, and 2) the process of growth and learning in the missionary enterprise is one of *action, reflection,* and *action,* that is, accomplishing missionary activity, analyzing the effectiveness of what has been done and making adjustments to allow for increased effectiveness, and then undertaking additional missionary activity.

From Luke's narrative we learn that: 1) discipleship requires growth and change, 2) the growth and change do not necessarily come easy, and that not all disciples grow and change at the same rate, 3) in the process of ongoing discipleship disagreements and challenges will arise, 4) sometimes debate is necessary, 5) solutions and resolutions to problems seldom come easily or quickly.

Discipleship: 1) involves times of reflection for the purpose of planning an effective contextualization strategy, 2) is rooted in missionary proclamation which will sometimes be well-received and sometimes not, 3) involves proclaiming a message that, even though it is contextualized, is essentially the same story told to all people so they can be reconciled to God.

Discipleship: 1) is an ongoing process of growth, 2) involves different levels of maturity and responsibility, 3) requires vigilance, 4) requires that the strong care for the weak, 5) involves struggle and sometimes danger, and 6) involves the sadness of separation, as some disciples are called to make great sacrifices.

According to Luke's picture of discipleship, the cost is high, the impact is pervasive, and the challenges are great. Two basic, recurring themes of the nature of discipleship seem to be 1) that it is missionary in nature and 2) involves a close connection to/with the Holy Spirit.

Discipleship In Luke-Acts

Having provided a brief overview of discipleship in Luke-Acts from a textual point of view, it may be helpful to reflect on the nature of discipleship from a more theological perspective.

On the Way With Jesus—A Radical Journey

Wilkins points out that disciples are followers of Jesus *"on the Way"* (1992:185). Before followers of Jesus were labeled by unbelievers as Christians (Ac.11:25), they were known as followers of the Way (Ac.9:1-2). Jesus referred to himself as *the Way* (Jn. 14:6). Discipleship is a way of life. It is living life as Jesus taught it ought to be lived. Therefore, following Jesus as we live our lives is being a disciple *on the way,* or *as we go.* Thus, Charles Van Engen entitled his book on mission theology, *Mission On The Way* (1996). Discipleship is being an apprentice of Jesus, living in relationship with him (Weder 1992:Vol. 2, 207-210) as we learn how to live properly in relation to God and to others.

Sweetland describes discipleship as a *journey* with Jesus (1990). It is another way of saying the same thing

Wilkins and Van Engen are saying: discipleship is following Jesus where he leads us in life. Where Jesus leads his followers today does not have so much to do with a physical location—though that may be a factor for those called to foreign mission service. For most followers of Jesus today, the journey is not to a geographic location, but to a relational location—to a closer relationship with God. And it is, in every sense of the word, a radical journey. For following Jesus into a closer relationship with God means being less like one's old sinful self and more like God. It is a transformational journey comprised of an intense relationship and a costly commitment.

An Intense Relationship

In Luke's Gospel, the journey with Jesus involves an intense relationship with him—a relationship that begins with a call to follow him.

The Call

When Jesus called Peter, James, and John, they left their fishing business and followed Jesus. When Jesus called Levi, he left his tax business and followed Jesus. Why did they do that? Because Jesus invited them to. He said, "Follow me." The invitation was personal. They would become his apprentices, following him, observing him, listening to him, learning from him. They would go with him, eat what he ate, sleep where he slept, experience that which he experienced. They would have a relationship with him, a relationship in which he would teach them, reshaping their perspective and their thinking. Jesus' call was not just a call to be trained to do a specific kind of work, but a call to be changed into a new kind of person. Any relationship that involves that kind of dynamic can be described as an intense relationship.

The Response

There is no such thing as a non-response to Jesus' call to discipleship. One responds positively, or one responds negatively. To be non-responsive to Jesus' call is, in effect, to respond negatively. The call to discipleship is an invitation into a relationship with Jesus. If that opportunity is not actively embraced, the invitation has been rejected. To fail to say yes to Jesus' invitation is to say no.

Luke's narrative includes both kinds of responses: positive and negative. Peter, James, John, Levi and many others responded positively, eagerly embracing the opportunity for a relationship with Jesus. The rich ruler, many of the religious leaders, and a large part of the mainstream Jewish population did not accept Jesus' call to discipleship.

Those who respond positively to Jesus' call to discipleship open themselves up to a radical reprioritizing of their lives and their values. They open themselves up to a new orientation in life, to a new perspective that alters their thinking and their behavior. Those who respond negatively say no to all those things.

A Costly Commitment

When people volunteered to follow Jesus or when he called them to be his disciples, he was very forthright about the "cost" involved (Lk. 9:57-62). Discipleship involved considerable sacrifice and commitment. Did they understand that? Could they follow through? If they were not going to be able to stick with it perhaps they should not begin.

During the days of Jesus' earthly ministry, following him was quite literal. Then, as we have seen, after Jesus returned to heaven and a literal kind of following was no longer possible, disciples "followed" him by following his way of life, his teachings. They adopted his perspective on

157

life. Did the cost of discipleship diminish after Jesus' ascension? Was it then easier to be his disciple? No. In fact, for some it may have been more difficult. To make a break with one's past as, for example, Levi did, allows one to distance himself from old habits, old ways of thinking and behaving. How much more difficult may discipleship have been for someone like Zacchaeus, who embraced Jesus' teachings and general lifestyle, yet who remained in the tax collection business? Zacchaeus had to deal with the demands of discipleship in the context of the tax collection business. Who faced the more difficult challenge, Levi or Zacchaeus? Some would say Zacchaeus.

Discipleship, then, did not become easier when it was no longer possible to literally follow Jesus from place to place during his earthly ministry. There was still a commitment to be made, a price to be paid. There were sacrifices to be made.

Sacrifice

What kind of sacrifice does Luke associate with the call to be a disciple of Jesus? The sacrifice of self. Luke includes Jesus' explanation of the kind of sacrifice he requires of his followers: *"If any of you wants to be my follower, you must put aside your selfish ambition, shoulder your cross daily, and follow me. If you try to keep your life for yourself, you will lose it. But if you give up your life for me, you will find true life,"* (Lk. 9:23-24). Jesus expects his followers to make the same kind of complete and completely selfless sacrifice he made in leaving heaven (Phil. 2:5-11).

Denying oneself, or as the New Living Translation words it, putting aside one's *selfish ambition,* is the greatest sacrifice one can make. It may even be a greater sacrifice than giving one's physical life. Those who sacrifice their physical lives for Jesus make the sacrifice and it is finished. Those who sacrifice (lay aside) their own self interests

158

continue to sacrifice over and over again. Each time they lay aside their own interests, goals, preferences, desires and will in favor of Jesus' interests, goals, preferences, desires and will they are sacrificing a significant part of their humanness—the drive to be self-fulfilling, self-determining, self-directed. There are not too many things more difficult to give up than the drive to be self-directed. But that is the price of discipleship. And Jesus made no apologies for demanding such a high price. Perhaps that is because he understood the reward associated with the sacrifice.

Reward

In Luke 18:18-28, Jesus assured his disciples that no one who made a sacrifice for the sake of the kingdom of God would go unrewarded. What reward did Jesus have in mind? Our first thought would most likely be the heavenly reward which awaits faithful believers. But could there be another perspective? I believe so. Since discipleship involves a close relationship between Jesus and his followers, the relationship itself can be thought of as a reward. What could be more rewarding than living life close to Jesus? What could be better than following him to the throne of God?

The work in which Jesus involves his followers can also be thought of as one of the rewards of discipleship. When Jesus called Peter, James, and John he told them he would teach them how to fish for people. That was the work they would do. Knowing they were participating with God in his mission in the world would have been deeply satisfying and rewarding for them. How would discipleship today be impacted if more believers thought of discipleship itself as their reward? Developing a deeper appreciation for what discipleship is may help people actually be better disciples.

The Christian Experience: Still a Radical Journey

Discipleship today is no different than it was in the first century—at least it shouldn't be. There is still a call to discipleship. Whenever the gospel is preached, Jesus invites people to become his followers. The invitation is the same. The cost and commitment remain the same. If there is a difference between disciples then and now it is related to how "radical" discipleship is. Words like radical, extreme and fanatic are not considered complimentary in our culture. You can believe just about whatever you want to believe in our society, as long as you keep it in check and don't become a fanatic. But many people would say that someone who walks away from a thriving business to pursue a new religious commitment is behaving in a radical manner. Turning your life upside down based on some new ideas you have come to espouse is considered extreme.

That's what discipleship is. It is the adoption of ideas that require radical changes in one's thinking and behavior. However, syncretistic processes have impacted contemporary Western Christianity to such a degree that most Western believers do not even realize how weak and watered down their discipleship is. Naturalistic materialism has impacted Western Christianity to such a degree that first century believers would have difficulty associating many churches today with the radical, dynamic community of faith in which they participated. The church today needs to rethink the demands of discipleship in light of Jesus' own sacrifice and the radical nature of discipleship as it is presented by Luke. Specifically, the church needs to rethink discipleship in terms of participation in a community of faith.

Participation in a Community of Faith

One of the main differences between the church of the first century and the contemporary Western church is the concept of community. Participation in a community of faith in the first century was very different than "going to church" today. It is essential that the idea of *going to church* be replaced with the concept of being a member of God's family, participating in family gatherings designed to honor our father, and in family activities designed to glorify him through service to others.

One of the reasons why community, in the true sense of the word, does not exist in the Western church today as it did in the first century church is our individualistic way of thinking and relating. People in the West are first and foremost individuals. We are not first and foremost part of a group. We are all related in some way to some kind of a group. We are part of a family. We have a group of friends. But our identity is not determined by any group. Who and what we are is rooted in our unique and individual personality. We are self-aware, self-possessed, self-determined individuals. *I think, therefore I am.*

People in non-Western cultures are not individualistically oriented. They are group oriented—part and parcel of their family and community. They have no frame of reference for existence apart from their group. Instead of saying *I think, therefore I am*, they would say, *I exist because we are.*

Christianity was born into a group oriented society. The community of faith became the group from which identity emerged and developed. Dedicated disciples had no frame of reference for life apart from the community of faith. How different this is from the Western concept of who one is in relation to the church. Discipleship in the contemporary Western church will never be like discipleship in the first century if we do not find a way to rethink our extreme individualistic orientation so we can begin to think of ourselves (understand our existence) as a part of a dynamic community of faith. How radical would that be?

Participation in God's Mission

Another of the main differences between the contemporary Western church and the church of the first century is our lack of a clearly defined purpose. Even in the larger Evangelical community who we are and what we are about is not entirely clear. And even those who are focused on the going and the telling (which is the proper focus) often view the entire operation as their own rather than a participation with God in his mission. Luke makes it clear that the mission is God's. The purpose is God's, the power is God's, the design and direction are God's. The church participates with God in *his* mission. We submit to him, adopting his purpose as our own—the reconciliation of all people. We become the conduit for his power, his love, his grace.

When the contemporary Western church is finally clear on who it is and what it is about (community and mission) contemporary discipleship will be as radical as it was in the first century.

Missiological Implications

What are the missiological implications of Luke's view of discipleship? There are several. I will mention only two, one in connection with foreign missions, and one in connection with local outreach.

First, as mission strategists plan for effective cross-cultural outreach the radical nature of discipleship must be kept clearly in mind. As the message is contextualized, it must not be compromised. Making the message easy to understand is not the same as making it easy to do. There is nothing easy about discipleship. The goal of context-ualization is a culturally appropriate presentation of the gospel, and culturally appropriate ways of living out one's faith. But even a culturally appropriate presentation of the Gospel is still the presentation of a concept that is in many respects quite radical. And a culturally appropriate response to that radical message is still a radical response. True discipleship is radical. It is life-altering. It is impossible to go into any society preaching a radical message which requires a radical response without causing some problems. We do not want to cause problems needlessly, or cause more problems than are necessary. But the changes required by Christian discipleship cannot be minimized in an effort not to cause ripples in the pond.

Second, since discipleship is by nature a missionary endeavor, local church leaders must plan and structure programs and activities so that opportunities for missionary (outreach) activities are abundant. Planning and structuring programs and missionary activities includes: 1) teaching that discipleship is a missionary endeavor, 2) training believers for different kinds of missionary outreach, and 3) giving them opportunities to use their newly acquired outreach skills. This can include short term mission trips into other cultures, local outreach across cultural and social boundaries, and participation in small groups designed for outreach and evangelism. These represent only a few of the more obvious activities that provide disciples an opportunity to be a disciple of Jesus—in the most complete sense of the word.

Summary

For Luke, discipleship is a journey with Jesus. It is a life commitment lived out *on the way*, that is, as we go through life with Jesus. It is a dynamic relationship with Jesus that allows us to be less like our old sinful selves and more like God. It is missionary in nature. The decision to follow Jesus is a radical, life-altering decision that requires the sacrifice of self (self-will, self-determination, self-centeredness) to the will of Jesus. Discipleship is not about acquiring a new skill. It is about becoming a new person—a new person who then helps others become new people.

Discipleship is costly. It requires sacrifice and commitment. It can be dangerous. In its pure form it is radical, extreme, and fanatical. It rarely exists in its pure form today—at least in the West. Syncretism has diluted contemporary Western discipleship so much that if first century believers found themselves in Western society today they would (in some instances) have trouble recognizing the church as the church.

Discipleship needs to be understood in terms of participation in the community of faith and in God's mission in the world, which is the reconciliation of all people. Disciples need to be reminded that they are, by nature, missionary people, and church leaders need to provide them with opportunities for missionary reflection and action. Missionary strategists need to be certain that in the process of contextualizing the message we do not compromise the demands of the message.

CHAPTER 5

MISSION AND EVANGELISM IN LUKE-ACTS: THE SPIRITUAL AND SOCIAL DYNAMICS OF HOLISTIC OUTREACH

What is the relationship between evangelism (the verbal presentation of the gospel) and holistic outreach? To a degree, the answer to that question depends on who is providing the explanation. My goal is to let Luke answer the question from his perspective. In Luke's mind, as far as we can tell, what is the relationship between evangelism and holistic outreach? Before proceeding to a study of Luke's text, it is necessary to clarify some terms.

Holistic Outreach

What is holistic outreach? It is balanced outreach that involves a proclamation of the Gospel as well as a demonstration of God's love and concern for every soul. It is seeing and ministering to the whole person. Bryant L. Meyers points out that "there can be no meaningful understanding of a person apart from his or her relationships—with God, self, community, those he or she calls 'other' and the environment. People, as individuals, are inseparable from the social systems in which they live," (1999:135). The components of holistic outreach include those concerns which are related to a holistic view of people. People are physical, emotional, intellectual, and spiritual. They exist in relation to God, to other people, and to their environment. For Myers, holistic outreach is outreach that involves the physical, emotional and intellectual aspects of an individual's life, as well as the spiritual.

Douglas McConnell explains:

> Holistic Mission is concerned with ministry to the whole person through the transforming power of the gospel. While holistic mission affirms the functional uniqueness of evangelism and social responsibility, it views them as inseparable from ministry of the kingdom of God. Therefore, holistic mission is the intentional integration of building the church and transforming society (2000:448-449).

Addressing the concerns of holistic outreach in more specific detail, Stuart Murray suggests that "concerns for peace, environmental action, human rights, liberation from oppression, material welfare, and a host of other possible dimensions of missions may be included" (2001:35).

Regardless of the specific dimensions one may attach to holistic outreach, it is an effort to view people holistically and to respond to them in the context of their lives. Holistic outreach certainly involves a specific verbal proclamation of the gospel, but is not limited to that medium of expression. Holistic mission is an attempt to combine the Great Commission and the Great Commandment into a single integrated holistic effort. It is proclamation combined with demonstration.

The Controversy Over Holistic Outreach

Not everyone is convinced of the importance, or even the theological correctness, of holistic outreach. George Peters' views are representative of many conservative believers.

> Most certainly Christians ought to be deeply involved in the social ills and struggles of society and to be energetically striving to bring reconciliation, remedy and assistance to mankind. Social welfare and advancement are significant and desirable; however, such services are not the mission of the church. Neither are they focal in the New Testament. New Testament Christian social ethics is personal, not ecclesiastical (1972:210).

David Hesselgrave agrees, suggesting that, "Christian missions is exclusive and specific and, that being the case, is particularistic and only in a secondary sense is it holistic," (1997).

The Arguments Against Holistic Outreach

Peters does not attempt to make a case for his assertions. He simply says that proclamation is the church's responsibility. On the one hand, he acknowledges a "service aspect" to the gospel as well as a proclamation aspect (1972:209), yet on the other hand he quotes Kerr, who denies the appropriateness of an integrated, holistic approach, suggesting that proclamation alone should be the Christian's focus (209). While Peters admits a social aspect to the gospel, he appears to be uncomfortable with it. His concern seems to be that we not allow ourselves to become unbalanced, focusing more on *social* than on *gospel*. In that concern Peters is correct. Balance is crucial. But that is exactly the point of an integrated holistic approach: balance in all things—especially as we demonstrate and proclaim our faith.

Hesselgrave, an opponent of holistic outreach, goes a step further than Peters. In one article he argues that as believers we must be holistic, demonstrating Christian love whenever possible, but that as missionaries we must be content to only proclaim the word (1997). His argument seems unnecessarily dichotomistic and reductionistic. How can one's responsibility as a believer to demonstrate God's love and care be divorced from one's proclamation of the gospel?

In another article, Hesselgrave argues that the poor in Luke 4:18-19 should not be understood in any literal sense (2003). His purpose appears to be to minimize the holistic aspect of Jesus' ministry. He suggests that the poor (*anawim*) of Isaiah's text be understood figuratively. If Isaiah's meaning was figurative, then, in Hesselgrave's view, Jesus' (and Luke's) meaning must also have been figurative. However, one wonders how the poor of Isaiah's day would have understood his message. Would not the poor, the brokenhearted, the captives, and the prisoners to whom Isaiah's message was directed have understood the Lord's promise in a literal way? They were looking for relief and the Lord was promising relief. Cyrus was used by God to provide that relief when he decreed that all displaced people could return to their ancestral homes. The people to whom Jesus spoke were well aware of that historical reality. Would they not have taken the promise the same way as the people of Isaiah's day?

It would be a mistake to ignore the spiritual aspects of what Jesus said. Relief for the poor, the brokenhearted, the captives and the prisoners includes spiritual relief. And of course, that is the most important aspect of Jesus' work. Jesus would free people from the bondage of sin. But it is a mistake to ignore the physical realities of the passage, especially in light of Jesus' ministry activities among the marginalized of Jewish society.

A complete overview of every position or argument in opposition to a holistic approach to mission or outreach is beyond the scope of this discussion. These two examples, however, are sufficient to demonstrate that not all theologians and missiologists would agree that holistic outreach is biblical and desirable. Rather than spending time reviewing what other theologians have said on the subject, considering what Luke has said would seem to be more appropriate.

Marginalized People in Luke-Acts

The place to begin in allowing Luke to direct our thinking regarding holistic outreach is in an analysis of his material related to marginalized people. Marginalized people in Luke-Acts are those people who do not enjoy the social status available to mainstream, socially acceptable people. Specifically, for Luke, marginalized people are women, children, the sick, the poor and the despised—that is, prostitutes, tax collectors and other "sinful" people. It is important 1) to understand how significant these marginalized people were to Luke, and 2) to then analyze specific acts of holistic outreach by Jesus and his followers as reported by Luke. First we will consider how Luke includes marginalized people in his two-volume work.

Luke 1:26-38

As an unmarried young woman, Mary would have had relatively low status in Jewish society. Being betrothed to a carpenter put her in the Jewish working class. She was not part of the very poor, but she was certainly not part of the influential ruling class. Her rights and opportunities were few. Yet it was to this inconspicuous young girl that the angel appeared with news about her role in the birth of the messiah. It is significant that God chose an insignificant young woman through whom he would come into the world. Why not a royal? Why not someone of the ruling class? Why not someone powerful and influential? God may have had many reasons why he chose Mary. Perhaps one of them was his interest in those who are not privileged.

Luke 1:39-55

During Mary's pregnancy she visited Elizabeth, who was also pregnant. During their greeting, Mary praised the Lord for what he had done in selecting her, his "lowly" servant. Was Mary simply being humble in referring to herself as lowly? Possibly. But it was also an accurate description given that she was a young woman. Socially, she was lowly. Even if she had been from a wealthy family, she was still just a young woman, a person of little influence (Summers 1972:32).

In her song of praise, Mary spoke of God as having exalted the lowly and satisfied the hungry while sending the rich away empty handed (vss. 52-53). If Mary was still speaking of herself, she was referring to God's choice of her over a rich, influential woman. God had blessed her and she was thankful. She understood herself as one of the lowly and was gratified that God had thought highly enough of her to select her when more socially suitable candidates were available.

To any first century woman (and to many today) reading Luke's gospel, God's choice of a single young woman from a working class family to serve as the vehicle by which he would bring his messiah into the world would have stood out as highly significant and unusual. What's the point? People not highly thought of by society are highly thought of by God.

Luke 2:8-14

The announcement of Jesus' birth to the shepherds in the fields focuses attention on another marginalized group: the shepherds. Douglas Oakman points out that those who worked the land and kept the sheep were part of the poor (*marginated*) working class (1991:164). The land and flocks were owned by the wealthy. The poor provided the labor. Why did God choose to announce the birth of Jesus to poor shepherds rather than the rulers of Jerusalem? Again, there may be many reasons why God did what he did. One reason, however, appears to be his interest in the marginalized of society. Those who have little in the way of social or economic power often respond to the gospel more eagerly and completely than those who are invested with material means. God is interested in marginalized people and marginalized people are often very interested in him.

Luke 2:21-24

While Joseph was not part of the very poor, he was certainly not wealthy. He was one of the working or craftsman class. However, when it came time to offer a sacrifice for Mary's first born, they offered the sacrifice of a poor couple, "a pair of turtledoves or two young pigeons," (see Lev. 12:8). Texts such as John 7:47-49 illustrate how low an opinion the Jewish authorities had of the common people. The uneducated, unsophisticated common people were, in the eyes of the ruling class, rabble, unworthy of serious consideration. It was within this class of people that God made his appearance as a human being. By intentional design he became one of the marginalized of society. Is it any wonder Jesus spent so much time among them?

Luke 2:36-38

How is this text about the prophecy of Anna related to Luke's interest in the marginalized of society? Anna was an old woman, a widow, who by today's standards might be classified as a religious fanatic. She was eighty-four years old and spent all her waking hours in the temple courts worshiping God in prayer and fasting. She was not a person of influence. She was not a teacher, a leader, or a benefactor. Few people, if any, sought her out to ask her advice. She was one of the many old women that someone had to take care of. She was part of the temple scenery, unnoticed by those who came and went—except for God. God was very aware of her. And he used her for his glory. Why? Because that's the kind of thing God does. He loves, rescues and uses society's throwaways. Old people, children, the sick, the poor, women: God loves and uses them in his kingdom to his glory. For God, there are no throwaways. Luke knows that and illustrates it over and over again as he tells his story.

Luke 3:10-11

Many of the crowds who came to hear John the Baptizer were part of the nameless rabble the Jewish leaders considered "sinners:" tax collectors, soldiers, unscrupulous businessmen, prostitutes, those who cared little for the strict purity rituals of the Pharisees. They were the common people, living common lives, sharing common problems and concerns. They were unimportant people whose opinions didn't matter, whose lives were inconsequential. But Luke's point is that there are no inconsequential lives. There are no lives that do not matter to God. Those who are unimportant to society are important to God. Those who are marginalized by society are centralized by God.

172

Luke 4:16-21

Fitzmyer provides an excellent technical analysis of this text (1970:525-539). Christopher Seitz (2001:309-552), John Watts (1987) and others provide excellent analyses of Isaiah's text, from which Jesus read as he addressed the Nazareth synagogue assembly. While most of the technical concerns associated with this text are beyond the scope of this study, one technical issue must be addressed: How would those listening to Jesus that day most likely have understood his words? They, much better than we, would have been aware of the original context of the Lord's message to his people through the prophet Isaiah. They would have understood the geopolitical and socioeconomic issues with which their ancestors wrestled centuries before. They would have understood the terms poor, captive, blind, and downtrodden (as expressed in the New Living Translation) in the full context of Isaiah's prophecy. They would have understood that third section of Isaiah's prophecy (for us chapters 55-66) to be about a captive and displaced people anticipating the fulfillment of God's promises, longing for relief, deliverance, forgiveness and re-establishment in their ancestral land, free of foreign oppression.

The Jews of Jesus' day lived with their own version of foreign oppression and dreamed of a day when God's promised messiah would appear, signaling a fulfillment of God's promises to them. In short, the people in the synagogue that day most likely would have understood Jesus' words in a very literal sense. Even Jesus' own followers understood the promises related to the messiah in a literal sense. It must be acknowledged, however, that their conceptions (or possible misconceptions) about what Jesus said cannot be the primary consideration in our interpretation of the text. The sociopolitical expectations of first century Jews regarding the nature and purposes of the messiah were in error. Jesus came to provide atonement for sin, not to overthrow the Roman government. A completely literal understanding of God's promises in Isaiah, fulfilled as God's displaced people returned to Jerusalem, or as Jesus fulfilled those promises as the messiah of God, misses the deeper spiritual implications of what God was doing for all people. Yet to spiritualize the entire text, denying any kind of "literal" fulfillment is to ignore the actual return of God's people from Babylonian captivity and the many ways in which Jesus literally changed people's lives by the way he interacted with them during his ministry. Whether he was giving sight to the blind, hearing to the deaf, life to the dead, health to the sick, food to the hungry, spiritual freedom to the spiritually harassed and oppressed, or lifted the spirits of the downtrodden by demonstrating God's love for them, much of what Jesus did in his ministry involved physically changing people's lives. Surely, given the things Jesus actually did during his ministry, Luke's words in this text must be understood both literally and spiritually.

Another consideration in understanding Luke's use of the Isaiah text is God's ongoing concern for marginalized people. Even a cursory reading of the Old Testament illustrates God's concern for the underprivileged and vulnerable of society. How many laws of the Sinaitic Covenant are designed to provide food and security for the poor? How often does God express his concern for the widow and orphan? How often does he, through the prophets, speak out against injustice and oppression of the weak? God's outrage at the mistreatment of marginalized people is especially clear in the prophecy of Amos.[17]

It is simply unthinkable to imagine God's outrage at the mistreatment of marginalized people while failing to understand his outrage at the failure of his people to

---

[17] Walter Pilgrim, David Seccombe, and S. John Roth have all done significant studies on the poor in Luke-Acts.

proactively reach out to the marginalized as a way of bearing his image to a world in need of reconciliation and hope.

Luke 6:20-26

This is another text that is often spiritualized to the point that there is no room for any kind of a "literal" understanding of what Jesus was saying. While it is important to note the futility of stacking up one list of scholars (who support one position) against another list (who support a different position), it is interesting to note that there are notable conservative scholars who understand Jesus' comments in this text in light of the socioeconomic realities of the day. Summers (1972:74) and Green (1997:266), to mention only two, understand the text in light of Luke's overarching concern for the marginalized of society, recognizing that Jesus' contrast between the poor and the rich has both literal and spiritual realities and ramifications. To ignore the physical realities and implications of poverty, hunger, sorrow and mistreatment in favor of a purely spiritualized interpretation of this passage, and of the gospel in general, is to ignore God's compassion for the suffering of his human children.

Luke 7:18-23

Here John the Baptist illustrates for us the power of preconceived notions. God had revealed to John that Jesus was *"the Lamb of God who takes away the sin of the world."* But when Jesus' actions did not match up to John's expectations of who the messiah would be and what he would do, John sent a delegation to inquire of Jesus if he was, in fact, the one sent from God. Jesus' response is interesting. As evidence that he was the one sent from God, Jesus said, *"the blind see, the lame walk, the lepers are cured, the deaf hear, the dead are raised to life, and the*

Good News is being preached to the poor." It would be difficult to successfully spiritualize this passage. Jesus had literally, physically done the things he spoke of. His ministry consisted of preaching the Good News *and* doing what he could to make a physical difference in people's lives. Perhaps this text should be utilized as a commentary on Jesus' use of the Isaiah text in the synagogue in Nazareth (4:16-21). For Jesus, making a difference in the lives of marginalized people was part of his work as the messiah of God. His approach to ministry was holistic.

Luke 7:36-50

There is nothing in this text to suggest that the woman in question was poor. In fact, she may have been a woman of means, since she brought a jar of expensive perfumed oil with which to anoint Jesus' feet. How, then, does she qualify as a marginalized person? She was a woman. And she was sinful. Perhaps she was a prostitute—which may explain how she was a woman of means. Regardless of her possible financial holdings, she was held in disdain by the Pharisee. She was not valued as a person. She was not merely a throwaway to be ignored, she was to be actively disavowed and denounced. To be sure, her sin needed to be denounced. But did her sin make her any less of a person than the Pharisee's sin made him less of a person? Was she worth less to God? Did she not deserve the same consideration as Simon? Did she deserve less respect than Simon simply because her sin was sexual in nature? Evidently Jesus did not think so. He responded to her the same way he responded to everyone else—with kindness and generosity of spirit. She was fully human and fully equal. She was interested in Jesus (and spiritual matters) and Jesus responded to her with compassion and forgiveness, offering her the dignity she deserved as one created in the image of God. How sad that the lesson seems lost on so many believers today.

Luke 8:1-3

Why would Luke specifically mention that a number of women, three mentioned by name, traveled with Jesus during his ministry? Why would he mention them so prominently along with the twelve? Is it possible that along with the twelve they were part of his ministry team? Whether they engaged in proclamation or not, as Green (following Witherington) notes, such prominent inclusion "would have been extraordinary" (1997:318). Why would Luke have done that? Because women were one of the groups of people who were marginalized in first century society. And part of what Luke is doing in his two-volume work is to highlight the fact that for God there are no marginalized people. All are of equal value and importance in his sight.

Luke 8:40-48

The focus in this text is on a young girl and an old woman. Both were sick. Neither enjoyed significant social status. As females they were marginalized. As sick people they were also marginalized. Because they were sick, contact with them involved issues of ceremonial uncleanness. Luke's Jewish readers would have been very aware of these factors. Jesus was aware of them as well. But he did not give them much weight. The young girl and the old woman were God's children, created in his image and in need of compassion and healing. That's all that mattered to Jesus. He responded to both as important human beings in need rather than as unimportant sick females.

Luke 16:19-31

The spiritual implications of the story of the rich man and Lazarus are clear and undeniable. The rich man was arrogant and did not seek out God. Lazarus was spiritually humble and depended on God. But to acknowledge that is not to deny the physical implications of the story. In fact, the story cannot be truly understood apart from the physical features of the story. Lazarus' reward in heaven stands in stark contrast to his pitiful physical circumstances in life. So, too, the rich man's suffering in hell is in contrast to the comfort he enjoyed in life. The physical realities are directly tied to the spiritual realities. The rich man's arrogance grew out of his riches. Lazarus' dependence on God grew out of his extreme poverty. To make their physical realities less real, less literal, is to eviscerate the story.

How does this text fit in with Luke's concern for marginalized people? After all, Lazarus' suffering in life was not relieved. His relief came afterward. Granted, Lazarus' relief was delayed, but he did eventually enjoy relief and reward. Luke's point is that even those who do not enjoy relief in this life are not forgotten by God. There is a special comfort awaiting those who suffer in this life—the comfort of being cradled in the Father's soothing embrace. Even if it may appear that God has forgotten, he has not. In the end, the marginalized will be emancipated, vindicated, and elevated by a loving Father who will right the wrongs perpetrated against the weak and vulnerable, against the ignored and forgotten.

Luke 18:1-8

The story of the persistent widow fits in well with Luke's overall focus on the marginalized. Will there be justice for those who have no power, wealth, or social status that will assure them of fair (to say nothing of privileged) treatment? The widow, though merely an old women, receives the justice she deserves because she is persistent. To be sure, her persistence is crucial to the process. But so is the judge's willingness to give her the justice she deserved even though she is not an influential person. She does not receive special treatment. She is treated equally. She is given the respect she deserves as a person—not any specific kind of a person, just a person. Her social status was not the issue. Her persistence and the judge's response were the issues. Even though the judge was not a kind, benevolent ruler who was eager to meet the needs of his people, she received justice. How much more will God, who is a kind and benevolent ruler, see that his people get justice—especially the marginalized who have no power to fend for themselves?

Luke 18:15-17

Children were marginalized in Jewish society. To group them among the marginalized does not mean that they were unloved. They were as cherished by their parents as any children in any society. But they had few (if any) rights. They had no social status or power. If there was a problem or a need, they could not handle it themselves. They needed a parent, guardian, or benefactor to serve as a mediator or advocate for them. On the ladder of social significance children occupied the lower rungs. In God's eyes, however, children occupy a position of tremendous importance. They are innocent and helpless. God is the champion and defender of the innocent and helpless. Jesus was not too busy to pause and bless the children. And God is not so occupied with running his world that he cannot pay attention to children—beautiful little humans who reflect his image much more brightly than do their adult counterparts.

Luke 19:1-10

Zacchaeus was a wealthy (and therefore powerful) Jewish man. How can he be classified as a marginalized person? Because he was a tax collector. He was considered a traitor—having sold out to the Romans for the opportunity to get rich by collecting taxes from his own people for the Roman oppressors. Zacchaeus was wealthy. He could buy what he wanted. But he was not a respected member of Jewish society. Wealth without the status and influence that usually accompany it is like a plane that can't fly. Could Zacchaeus ever enjoy the status of a successful person? In Jewish society, no. But in God's kingdom, yes. That is Luke's point. Those who are despised by others are loved and appreciated by God.

Luke 21:1-4

The story of the widow's offering is a powerful illustration of the significant role marginalized people can play in the kingdom of God. In the story, who actually contributed more, the wealthy men or the poor widow? Proportionately, the widow gave more because she gave all she had. Jesus elevated the status of that poor widow above that of the wealthy, influential men. In what realm is that sort of thing possible? In the spiritual realm of the kingdom of God. Luke's point would not have been lost on his original readers. Life in the kingdom of God is a very different sort of thing than life in the world. In God's kingdom the lowly are lifted high. No wonder the lowly respond so readily.

Acts 2:44-46

People in need are marginalized people. Not having enough food or clothing or a place to stay, or the means to procure those necessities, places one outside the bounds of productive, responsible, acceptable society. How does a group of people who are able to provide for themselves deal with a group of people who cannot? A number of the "Haves" can make a small donation to individual "Have Nots," thereby relieving some of the distress. Or those who have can eagerly embrace those in need seeing that their needs are met. This is what happened in Jerusalem following the events of Pentecost of AD 30. Believers of means provided for the needs of believers who were unable to provide for themselves. The needs of the marginalized in the new community were met.

Luke does not deal with the issue of the needs of the marginalized within the community of faith versus those outside the community. Paul suggested simply that we be ready to help anyone who needs help, especially those who are fellow believers (Gal. 6:10). This is what the believers in Jerusalem were doing. They were so concerned to help that they made extraordinary sacrifices, selling property in order to have funds to supply the needs of the poor among them.

Acts 3:1-10

While the believers in Jerusalem were especially aware of the needs of their own community, they did not consider those not yet a part of their community of faith to be beyond the reach of their generosity. The crippled beggar was truly one of society's marginalized, brought to one of the temple entrances each day (to the Beautiful Gate) to beg from those coming and going. While Peter and John had no money to give the man, they were willing to do what they could. What they were able to do was worth more than any amount of money they could have given him. Contemporary Western believers tend to throw money at just about any problem that comes along. Money is not always the best or most appropriate solution.

It is important to note that while the focus of Luke's narrative has shifted and, relatively speaking, not as much attention is concentrated on the marginalized in Acts as it is in the Gospel, the marginalized were still present and believers continued to meet their needs however they could.

Acts 4:32

This text represents another instance (or perhaps an ongoing effort) on the part of believers to meet the needs of the poor within their community of faith. We do not know when the events described by Luke in this text occurred— whether six weeks or three years after the events of Pentecost. Whatever the timeframe, these events occurred after the events referred to in Acts 2:44-46 (Bruce 1954:108-109), and represent an additional effort.

Acts 6:1-7

This text represents another instance of financial aid being directed toward the marginalized. Hellenistic widows in the new community of faith were in need. They were marginalized because 1) they were women, 2) they were widows, and 3) they were Hellenistic (rather than Palestinian). The community of believers responded to their needs—at first not so well, but then quite purposefully. Again, this is an instance of responding to the marginalized who were part of the community of faith, rather than a response to the marginalized not yet part of the community. However, the point is that the new community of faith was sensitive to material needs and was willing to meet them, so much so that they appointed special servants to be responsible for the needs. And, as is apparent from Acts 3:1-10, when confronted with the needs of those not yet part of the community, the believers responded as effectively as they could. Their approach to mission and ministry was clearly holistic.

Acts 10:1-48

Why this text would be included in a discussion of holistic outreach may not immediately be clear. After all, Peter and his fellows Jews did not offer Cornelius any kind of material assistance. There was no reason for them to. Being a Centurion, Cornelius was a man of means—at least he was not needy. However, was there a group more marginalized by Jews than the Gentiles? A Gentile person had no status at all in the eyes of a Jew. Luke's point, however, is that marginalized people matter to God. Who or why or to what degree one is marginalized is not the point. One can be wealthy (like Zacchaeus) and still marginalized. Cornelius was an influential man in his own social group. In Jewish society he was lower than low. In the new community of faith, however, he was an equal. Reaching out to him, which included going into his home and having table fellowship with him was, from a typical Jewish perspective, more costly than even a significant charitable donation would have been. But after God's prompting, Peter was willing to broaden his view of mission and ministry to include even the most marginalized—non-Jewish people.

The balance of the book of Acts contains many instances of holistic outreach to marginalized people. Enough have been noted to make the point: God cares about marginalized people and outreach must include demonstration as well as proclamation. Holistic outreach is balanced outreach to all people. It is not only about the material needs of the poor. It is about the needs of people— physical, emotional, intellectual, social, spiritual—whatever needs they may have. It is about ministering to the needs of people created in the image of God. Luke's two-volume work includes numerous instances of holistic outreach because Luke understood God's interest in all people—especially those marginalized by society.

Holistic Outreach in Luke

This section will consist of a brief overview of each of the incidents recorded by Luke which demonstrate Jesus or his followers engaging in holistic outreach. In the previous section the focus was on Luke's interest in various groups of marginalized people. This section will focus on how the needs of marginalized people were met.

Luke 4:31-36

Why did Jesus drive away the demon that was harassing the man in this text? Was it merely to demonstrate his power over the supernatural forces of evil and gain a more sympathetic hearing from his audience? Some have suggested that Jesus' supernatural acts were merely for that purpose. While it is clear that the supernatural things the Holy Spirit empowered Jesus to do did generate curiosity and interest, and in many cases belief, there is nothing in the text to suggest that the sole motive (on the part of Jesus or the Holy Spirit who empowered him) was to get attention and demonstrate power. Certainly those were results. But to suggest that they were the sole motive is simply unwarranted. Matthew says that Jesus healed the sick because he felt compassion for them (Mt. 14:4). Jesus drove away demons because he felt compassion for those being tormented by evil spiritual powers.

It is interesting that as Luke records this incident of holistic outreach he does not suggest that the healing is in any way conditional on listening to Jesus preach about the kingdom of God. It is likely that the man would have been keenly interested in listening to Jesus. But the healing was offered without condition.

Luke 4:38-31

In this text, the marginalized people include a specific reference to Peter's mother-in-law, and the more general references to "the sick" and "the demon possessed." Jesus healed the sick and drove away demons. While his willingness to help does not appear to be conditional on their willingness to listen, Jesus was clearly focused (as versus 42-44 make clear) on preaching his message of Good News about the kingdom. It is important that any discussion regarding holistic outreach pay careful attention to balance between proclamation and demonstration. Jesus' reason for coming into this world was to provide atonement for sin. His message was rooted in that reality. No matter how many people he healed in the process, no matter how many marginalized people he responded to, or in what ways he responded to them, his overarching goal was always to glorify God and reconcile the lost. However, in that context he was clearly interested in meeting people's needs, regardless of what they were. His was a balanced, holistic ministry.

Luke 5:12-16

In this example of holistic outreach, Jesus was so concerned about meeting the leper's needs that he did an extraordinary thing. He touched the man. Jesus did not need to touch the man to heal him. But the man needed to be touched. His leprosy had made him quite literally untouchable—perhaps for many years. His lack of human contact may have been the most painful aspect of his condition. He needed not just to be healed, but to be reconnected to humanity, to be relieved of the pain of isolation. He needed physical contact with another person. Jesus was willing to give him that which he had done without for so long. The man did not ask Jesus to touch him.

He asked only for healing. Jesus was willing to give the man that which he needed, even though the man had not specifically asked for it. It was an example of holistic outreach.

We know what people truly need. They need to hear the gospel and be saved. We cannot allow that most important need to get lost in the myriad of so many other needs that are ultimately less important. However, neither can we ignore the other important needs people have. We need to "touch" the marginalized with the love of God.

Luke 5:17-26

In this instance, the man's physical and spiritual healing were connected. When the paralyzed man was lowered in front of Jesus and those who had crowded into the house, Jesus pronounced his sins forgiven. Jesus went on to explain that his choice of words had been intentional so that the religious leaders would know that he had the power to forgive sins. Then Jesus told the man to get up, pick up his mat and go home because he was healed. Jesus did not explain the exact relationship between the forgiveness and the healing, but that they were somehow connected seems clear. Sometimes the healing people need (especially inner healing) comes attached to the forgiveness they receive when they respond to the Gospel. Whether it is our method of outreach, or God's response to the person's faith, the needs of the whole person are important. Holism is a divine invention not a human invention.

Luke 6:6-11

Many of the things Jesus did, such as healing people on the Sabbath, resulted in controversy. Did Jesus heal the man with a deformed hand on the Sabbath in order to create a controversy so he could point out the hardheartedness and hypocrisy of the religious leaders? Or did he heal the man because he had compassion on the man and wanted to help him whether or not his actions resulted in controversy? Suggesting that Jesus behaved in controversial ways in order to create a dialog borne of conflict may, for some people, be problematic. To suggest, however, that Jesus was willing to put people's needs ahead of tradition, theology, and the expectations of the religious leaders is entirely satisfactory. Why was Jesus willing to put people's needs ahead of what we might refer to as *political correctness*? Because people created in the image of God deserve to be given every possible consideration.

Luke 7:1-10

The key to understanding the significance of this text is Jesus' willingness to go with the man to his house—even though the man was a Gentile and to enter his house would have rendered Jesus ceremonially unclean. In Jewish society, that Roman officer was as marginalized as a person could be. Yet Jesus was willing to respond to his need. Of course, the Roman officer and Jesus were only two of the three people involved in this human triangle. The sick slave was the third. Not only was Jesus willing to help the Roman officer, but to help him by healing his slave, another even more marginalized person. The officer, at least, was a man of rank and respect. His slave was another matter. The slave's rank, however, did not matter to Jesus. He was willing to give what he had to give to those in need regardless of their social status.

Luke 8:26-39

This account of exorcism differs from the previous account (4:31-36) in that Jesus encourages the man to go and proclaim all the wonderful things God has done for him.

The power and love of God is magnified as the man tells his story over and over again. People come to know that God is not distant and uncaring, but close, and willing and able to intervene, making a difference in the quality of one's life. The point is not only that God is more powerful than Satan, but that he is willing to use his power to our benefit. He loves us. And while the nature of life in this world as he has created it is such that he cannot eliminate all suffering, he is, in a number of ways, willing to intervene and make things better. One of the primary ways he intervenes is through his people and the good deeds they do in his name. There is more to being God's image bearers in the world than verbal proclamation. The Great Commission and the Great Commandment cannot be separated.

Luke 8:40-56

On his way to help a young girl, Jesus was delayed by an old woman. Jesus patiently, compassionately dealt with the old woman's needs. By the time he arrived to help the young girl, she had died. Jesus raised her back to life. His power is greater than death, extending into the realm of the unseen. These are the facts as Luke has recorded them. But what is the significance of the facts in the context of our discussion? Neither the young girl nor the old woman enjoyed social prominence. Simply because of who they were, they were marginalized people. They were also people who needed help. Jesus helped them. What more needs to be said?

Luke 9:10-17

Jesus had been teaching the crowds, meeting their spiritual needs by teaching them about the kingdom of God. But people are not only spiritual beings, they are also physical beings. So in time the crowds' physical needs became a concern—they became hungry. Jesus did not suggest that he was there to meet their spiritual needs and that their physical needs were their own responsibility or the responsibility of the governmental leaders. Jesus fed the people. Did he do so only to make a point: that God can supply one's physical needs? If Jesus' point was only to make a point, what would have been the point? If Jesus was not really concerned about the people's physical needs, what difference did it make that God could meet their physical needs? Jesus fed hungry people because he cared about their needs. He taught them and he fed them—holistic outreach.

Did Jesus feed everyone he taught? No. Did he heal everyone he encountered who needed healing? Probably not. Did he change the physical circumstances of everyone he encountered? No. Can we? No. But does that realization relieve us of the obligation to do what we can to help people when and where we can? It does not.

Luke 9:37-43

This text includes another episode of exorcism. The victim of the demon was a young man. We do not know whether he was nine or nineteen. In that culture, a young man could still be called a "boy" if he was in his twenties. Jesus' disciples could not drive the demon away and this annoyed Jesus. They should have had enough faith to control the evil spirit. They did not, so Jesus stepped in and did what they had been unable to do. How is this text an illustration of holistic outreach? Jesus did for the young man that which his disciples could not do. They wanted to help, but couldn't. Jesus had the power they lacked, and was willing to use it. There was never a question as to whether the young man should be helped. He had a need. Jesus met his need. There is not so much as a hint that Jesus felt his job was proclamation only and that people's other needs (beyond the need to hear the Gospel) were not a vitally important part of his mission to glorify God while saving the lost.

Luke 13:10-17

Again Jesus was faced with helping a woman who desperately needed help or withholding his assistance in order to comply with the assumptions and traditions of the religious establishment. Clearly, Jesus was not only concerned about the woman's soul. He could have preached the Good News in that synagogue and not annoyed the leaders by healing the woman. He could have waited until sundown and healed her then, after the Sabbath was over. It appears, however, that for Jesus, preaching the Good News included a component of God's love and care for his human children.

Part of what made the Good News about the kingdom of God good was God's presence and the exercise of his power in people's lives. When God is present, life is better. This does not mean that everyone's problems are automatically solved, that all suffering is relieved and life becomes a spiritual and physical utopia. But it does mean that God's presence makes a positive difference. How could Jesus illustrate that without impacting people's lives in a concrete way? He couldn't. So as Jesus preached he healed, he exorcised, he blessed, he touched, he fed, he resurrected, he loved, he encouraged. He changed people's lives. He touched the woman in the synagogue and healed her. The touch and the healing were part of his message. Something similar must also be part of our message. We may not heal people as Jesus did, but we must find concrete ways to demonstrate the love we are talking about as we preach the Good News. Jesus' approach was holistic and ours must be as well.

Luke 14:1-6

This Sabbath controversy is nearly identical to the previous incident described in 13:10-17. Luke may have arranged them in such close proximity in an effort to strengthen his presentation of Jesus as one willing to incur the wrath of the religious establishment rather than allow human needs to go unmet—even for a day. The needs of the marginalized were more important than the assumptions and traditions of the establishment. Jesus would minister to the whole person whether or not the religious leaders liked it.

Luke 17:11-19

This text provides us with an interesting insight into one aspect or result of holistic outreach: glory to God. When Jesus healed the ten lepers, one returned, praising God for his healing. Jesus was saddened that only one of the men—a Samaritan—returned to thank him and praise God, but he was happy that through at least one of the men God was being glorified. When God's people do good things, empowered and enabled by the Holy Spirit who lives in us, God is glorified. The combination of proclamation and demonstration is the most effective form or method of communication. Perhaps this is why Luke opened the book of Acts with a reference to all that Jesus began to *do and teach* (Ac.1:1)—proclamation and demonstration combined to become a more effective form of communication than either one of them alone could have been.

Luke 18:35-43

Why did Jesus perform this supernatural act, giving sight to the blind man? At this point in his ministry it would be difficult to explain it as an attempt to demonstrate his power. His power is no longer in question. The blind man

191

requested that Jesus heal him because he was completely convinced that Jesus had the power to do so. Was Jesus merely trying to gain a hearing? Obviously not. Stopping to talk with the man was an interruption. Why, then, did Jesus stop and talk to the man? And why did he grant the man's request to be able to see? Because Jesus cared about the man, and because he could make a difference in the man's life. Jesus' holistic view of ministry and outreach included helping when and how he could.

Holistic Outreach in Acts

As mentioned above, Luke began the letter we refer to as Acts by referring to all that Jesus began to *do and teach*. That combination of demonstration and proclamation was the most effective form of communication Jesus could use to accomplish his mission in the world. Luke began this way because his interest in marginalized people and holistic outreach is not confined to his Gospel. While he has much to accomplish in the book of Acts, he still dedicates many texts to the issue of marginalized people and holistic outreach.

Acts 3:1-11

This text was examined in a previous section focusing on the presence of marginalized people in Luke's material. The reason for noticing it again is to focus attention on the fact that as Luke continued part two of his presentation he continued to be concerned about marginalized people, as did the community of believers about whom he is writing. Just as Jesus had practiced a holistic form of ministry and outreach, so did his followers. Peter did not tell the beggar that he had no money to give him and then proclaim the Gospel to the man. Peter told the man that he had no money to give him, but that he would do for him what he could. And then Peter healed him.

Holistic ministry and outreach does not have to involve money. Jesus did not have money to give people, or money to finance various kinds of social services. He cared about people and did for them that which the Holy Spirit empowered him to do. The same can be said of Peter, John and the first century community of believers. Holism does not equal money. Holism equals love and concern and a willingness to do what the Holy Spirit has empowered one to do. Perhaps much of the concern over holistic outreach is that we have not opened ourselves up to what the Holy Spirit can empower us to do.

Acts 4:32-37

Several features of this text are crucial in analyzing the success of those early believers. First, they were unified. Second, they took care of one another, including physical needs, selling property as needed to fund the food and shelter needs of the poor in the community of faith—so much so that in the Jerusalem community there was no one whose needs were not met. Third, the apostles provided powerful witness concerning the resurrection of Jesus. The combination of a unified community of faith proclaiming and illustrating the Good News was an unbeatable combination. Satan could do nothing to stop them or even diminish their efforts. Their concern for the marginalized of society, both in and out of their community of faith, was a powerful testimony to the goodness of the Lord they served.

Acts 5:12-16

Healing and exorcism continued to be key activities (along with other kinds of supernatural activities) in the holistic outreach and ministry in that first community of believers. They were not only concerned about the needs of fellow believers, but continued to do good to anyone who needed help. As a result, the community of faith continued to grow. This raises some important questions: were the supernatural activities/events accomplished by the Holy Spirit through the apostles done simply to demonstrate that there was power behind the message and that the message, therefore, ought to be heeded? Or were the supernatural events part of the church's holistic outreach designed to demonstrate the love of God and the availability of his power to impact people's lives? In other words, was God saying, "I have amazing power so you had better listen to me"? Or was he saying, "I love you and I'm willing to use my power to impact your life in a positive way"? I believe the second option is preferable.

Acts 8:4-8

This text is especially helpful in demonstrating that the early believers were very open to the various groups of marginalized people. The Samaritans were among the most marginalized people in that part of the world at that time. John tells us that the Jews had no dealings with the Samaritans (Jn. 4:9). But that statement alone does not explain the reasons or extent of the animosity. Dollar provides a brief summary of scholarly views on how the Jews thought of the Samaritans (1990:111-114). Regardless of how the debate over the Jewish view of the Samaritans may be resolved, the reality is that the Samaritans were marginalized people. Yet, Philip, a Jewish believer, went to them with the Good News about Jesus. The sick were healed. Those harassed by demons were freed from that oppression. God's love for the Samaritans was demonstrated to them in concrete ways and they responded. To what did they respond? To the Good News. But how was that Good News communicated? In word *and* deed; by proclamation *and* demonstration. Philip's approach to mission was holistic.

Acts 9:32-35

It does not appear that Aeneas was a believer. Peter, engaging once again in holistic outreach, healed him and as a result many people in the area became believers. What motivated them? Was it merely that Peter had an amazing source of power at his disposal, and because of that the people believed his message? Or was it that God's power was used to impact a man's life in a beneficial way? Demonstrations of power for the sake of demonstrating power stem from a deep seated insecurity that manifests itself in a need to impress or intimidate. Does that sound like the way God works? Or is it better to suggest that a God of infinite power and love expresses his power in loving actions? Peter was not simply demonstrating how powerful God was. He was engaged in holistic outreach.

Acts 9:36-41

Tabitha (or Dorcus) provides us with a marvelous example of a believer who had a holistic perspective of ministry and outreach. *"She was always doing kind things for others and helping the poor,"* (vs. 36). Many of the widows who had experienced her kindness first hand were there to explain to Peter how her love had touched their lives. They mourned her loss. We do not know how many of them had become believers because of her holistic outreach, but that God had been glorified by her many acts of kindness is obvious. Holistic outreach provides an avenue for the lost to be saved while God is being glorified.

Acts 19:11-12

The same kind of abilities evident among the apostles (especially Peter, Ac. 5:14-16) in the earliest days of the faith were utilized by Paul many years later in Ephesus. Why? Not merely as a demonstration of power, but as an expression of God's willingness to use his power to impact people's lives in a positive way. It is another example of holistic outreach utilized by early believers to reach the lost while glorifying God.

Acts 28:7-10

Again we see Paul using his power to heal to help others and to glorify God. Luke does not tell us of any proclamation that occurred, but it is unimaginable that Paul would not have spoken to the people of Malta about the resurrected Lord. Surely his demonstrations of God's power and love were coupled with his proclamation concerning faith in the resurrected Lord.

The Spiritual and Social Dynamics of Holistic Outreach

What happens when the church practices holistic outreach? The combination of proclamation and demonstration creates a dynamic interaction between the spiritual and social realities of life that puts God right at the center of human existence—where he belongs! Individuals (or communities) who experience holistic outreach experience God more fully than those who receive only proclamation or only demonstration. The combination of proclamation and demonstration as the most complete communication of God's message creates a spiritual and social dynamic that would not otherwise exist. The spiritual blessings of atonement, forgiveness, indwelling and hope spring to life more fully and completely in individuals and communities as a result of hearing *and* seeing the Good News about Jesus. So too, the social blessings of peace, harmony, brotherhood, love and respect for others, and increased moral and ethical awareness develop more completely in a society as a result of hearing *and* seeing the Good News about Jesus.

The word of God spoken and the love of God lived create an energy, in a single life or in a community of lives, that allows for more complete change more quickly and more thoroughly than would otherwise be possible. Holism is a dynamic process. The combination of proclamation and demonstration generates a spiritual and social energy that facilitates more effective mission and evangelism.

Summary

Luke's entire work is laced with references to and examples of outreach to marginalized people. The poor, the sick, the oppressed, the old and forgotten, women, children, tax collectors and sinners, Samaritans and Gentiles: all are given prominent places in Luke's two-volume work. His focus is not only on what Jesus taught, but on what Jesus did. The same is true for Jesus' followers. What they taught is important. But so is what they did. And what they did, as did Jesus, was practice holistic outreach, holistic mission and ministry.

A basic consideration in analyzing the appropriateness of a holistic approach to mission and evangelism is the maintenance of a proper balance between proclamation and demonstration. Without balance one ends up on opposite ends of the gospel spectrum. On one end there is the social gospel—all demonstration but no proclamation. On the other end there is the verbal gospel—all proclamation but no demonstration. Either extreme results in a one dimensional (and therefore a skewed version) of God's multifaceted communication to his human children regarding his love, his desire for a relationship, and his offer of grace and mercy, which if accepted, will result in reconciliation and salvation. Balance is absolutely imperative in holistic outreach. In fact, without balance there can be no holistic outreach, for that which results in a holistic approach is a balance between proclamation and demonstration.

CHAPTER 6

THE MISSIOLOGICAL IMPLICATIONS OF LUKE-ACTS FOR THE CHURCH TODAY

We have covered a great deal of ground thus far in our discussion of Luke's work. His authorial perspective was both historical and theological. Our perspective has been missiological. And although Luke did not think in terms of the contemporary discipline of missiology, his theological perspective was clearly rooted in his understanding of the *missio Dei*. For Luke, the fulfillment of God's mission in the world through the ministry of Jesus (which is the reconciliation of all people) is the heart and soul of a vital, living theology. One might even suggest that Luke's theology is so rooted in the *misso Dei* that it is impossible to discuss Luke's theology thoroughly and accurately without discussing mission.

That being the case, it is important that we attempt to analyze, at least in a basic way, the missiological implications of Luke's work for the contemporary community of faith. In this chapter, I will offer a few thoughts on each of the five preceding chapters in an attempt to highlight the basic missiological issues with which the local church today must be concerned. In many ways, the church at the local level is what "the church" is. So in what way does Luke's theology—his missiology—confront or impact the local church?

Developing a Universal Perspective in Local Churches

Chapter 1 dealt with Luke's intentional movement from a particularistic Jewish context to a universal context. He began his story in one place and ended it in a very different place. Why did he do that? To demonstrate to both Jews and non-Jews that while the Jews held a very prominent place in God's plan for reconciling the world to himself, the reconciliation was available to all people. It was available to all people, regardless of their social status (whether or not they were marginalized) and regardless of their ethnic origins (whether or not they were Jewish). Proclaiming the universal nature of the Gospel was Luke's intent.

But surely everyone today understands that the Gospel is universal in nature. The Gospel is for all. Luke's point is clearly understood so we can move on to other issues. Can we? Are we sure that at the local church level Luke's point is so clearly understood? Perhaps Luke's point is understood on a theoretical level. But in how many churches does it appear to have been embraced in any meaningful, practical way? How many local churches truly see themselves as a local branch of the universal, missional church given the specific responsibility to reach out to all people? Is this not the issue Darrell Guder and others have addressed in their work, *Missional Church: A Vision for the Sending of the Church in North America*? Their observation is that the church's "problem. . . has to do with [a failure to recognize] who we are and what we are for" (1998:3).

We are God's reconciled people invited to participate with him in his mission of reconciliation of all people. While I do not have specific statistical data to support my contention, I will suggest that it appears obvious to more than just a few missiologists that local churches in general do not see themselves as directly responsible for carrying out the Great Commission. Why not? At least one reason may be that local ministers (even in evangelical churches) have not spent adequate time preaching about the universal scope of God's plan and how local churches are expected to be involved in that endeavor.

Gailyn Van Rheenen and Bob Waldron conducted a survey that, among other things, measured the relationship between a local church's involvement in missions and how many times each year the pulpit minister preached about missions. 53% of the churches surveyed said their preacher spoke about missions one to three times per year. 22% said their pulpit minister preached about missions four to six times per year. 3% said their pulpit minister preached on mission work seven or more times per year. Van Rheenen and Waldron concluded, "The survey showed a direct correlation between the congregation's involvement in missions and the frequency of preaching on world outreach. The more the preacher spoke on outreach themes, the greater was the perception that the church was deeply involved in missions," (2002:46).

It seems clear that one of the ways to help believers in local churches understand their need to be involved in outreach (local and global) is regularly scheduled preaching about outreach that is specifically aimed at increasing involvement at the local level. Believers in local churches must learn to see the universal scope of God's plan, but to see it in relation to their local context. This is the point of Charles Van Engen's book, *God's Missionary People: Rethinking the Purpose of the Local Church* (1991). The local church is part of God's universal church and is to be an active participant with God in his mission in the world. Local believers (churches) need to send missionaries. But local believers also need to be missionaries in their own community. Regularly scheduled preaching designed to teach and motivate regarding local outreach is essential if believers in the local church are to have a locally realized universal perspective.

Beyond understanding the role of the local church in God's universal plan of reconciliation, believers in local churches need to be active in local outreach. Leaders can assist them in living out their faith in meaningful ways by providing opportunities and avenues for outreach. It is not enough to teach and motivate believers regarding local outreach. Leaders must provide ways and means for believers to do what they are being asked to do. Leaders must think creatively and design (dare we use the dreaded "P" word?) *programs* to make it less challenging (and/or intimidating) for believers to engage in effective holistic outreach. The simple reality is that if believers feel the challenge before them is too complicated or beyond their abilities, they will not attempt it. Local church leaders must be sensitive to the perceived limitations of believers in their churches and do everything possible to minimize the difficulties and challenges believers have to overcome as they attempt to participate with God in his mission in the world.

It is not my purpose here to suggest specific programs of outreach for local churches. That which works in one church context may not work in another. Instead, local leaders need to scrutinize and analyze their community to see what needs exist and how the church might go about addressing those needs holistically. The key in this process is for leaders to be visionary (in the sense of seeing what can be) and thinking creatively and innovatively in designing ways for the church to make a difference in people's lives. These may include things like "special life-situation ministries," (Morris 1993:162) such as divorce recovery, substance abuse, shelter and counseling for victims of physical abuse, homeless shelters, pregnancy crisis, new immigrant language classes, after school programs, literacy programs, food assistance programs, school supplies for low income families, tutoring for primary and secondary school children, money management seminars, seniors transportation. On and on the list could go. The point is to: 1) identify the specific needs that exist in a community, and 2) design programs that will provide believers with a realistic way of participating in meeting those needs.

In doing this, the old saying, "See It Big, Keep It Simple" is a good guiding principle. Complexity is not inherently evil, but unnecessary complexity can kill a program before it has a chance to work.

Helping believers in local churches develop a universal perspective includes helping them understand that God's universal plan for all people begins at each local church with individual believers making a difference in the lives of the people around them. Helping believers develop a universal perspective also includes providing them with avenues of opportunity so they can put their universal perspective to work in a meaningful way.

Developing A Missional Perspective In The Local Church

It is clear from Luke's Gospel that Jesus came here with a specific mission in mind. It is not necessary at this point to argue the case for the missional nature of the church. The case has been made: *the church is God's reconciled people who are sent into the world to tell the story of Jesus so others can believe and be reconciled to God. The* missio Dei *is the reconciliation of all people. God's reconciled people are to participate with him in his mission in the world.* His mission becomes our mission. Most Christians understand this. But many local churches seem to have

203

difficulty translating what they *know* into what they *do*. How does a local church go about developing a missional perspective that is lived out in the day-to-day life of that church?

There are two basic things church leaders can do to help local believers develop a missional perspective. First, there must be intentional, specific teaching about the missional nature of the church and her mission in the world. Teaching in local churches must be balanced. We must teach people to *observe all the things that Jesus commanded*, but we must do so within the larger context of preparing people to go out and tell the story of Jesus. Felt needs must be addressed in local churches. Nurturing of believers must be holistic and thorough. Ministry in local churches must be designed to meet the needs of people who are struggling to be who and what God wants them to be. *But all of that must be done in the context of preparing believers to go out into the world to participate with God in his mission.* Every sermon preached, every class taught, every program initiated must be evaluated in light of the church's ultimate purpose: participation with God in his mission in the world. Specific, intentional teaching about the nature of the church and what that means for individual believers must permeate the preaching and teaching in the local church. The subject cannot be the directly addressed all the time. But it can be the underlying foundation upon which the preaching and teaching of a church are built. This is not to say that Christological and Soteriological issues are not at the heart of what we preach and teach. Jesus is the foundation of everything. But the reason for the incarnation and Jesus' sacrifice of atonement was to make possible the reconciliation of all people. That was (and remains) God's purpose in all he has done. Preaching rooted in the life and death of Jesus cannot be separated from teaching about the missional nature of his church.

Since much of the teaching that occurs in local churches is accomplished in the form of lectures, special attention must be given to group discussion. Group discussion involves a dynamic that allows for concepts to be clarified and solidified. It allows for a dynamic interchange that assists people in adjusting their thinking and getting comfortable with a new idea. It is unrealistic to expect that believers will simply embrace an idea that requires changes in their thinking and behavior because they have heard a few sermons or attended a few classes on the subject. They need time to discuss it and get comfortable with the idea.

Second, in addition to specific and intentional teaching and discussion on the missional nature of the church, church leaders need to engage in discipling that allows believers to engage in activity that is missional in nature. Some people have a gift for reaching out to and helping others. Most don't. For most of us, outreach is difficult. Anything church leaders can do to make it easier is helpful. Ministry structures within local churches designed to provide believers with opportunities for outreach, combined with the companionship of a mature believer to model and encourage holistic outreach, enhances the likelihood that believers will develop a missional perspective as well as an appreciation of and the requisite skills for effective outreach.

It is amazing how many evangelical churches do not have a missional perspective. How is that possible? Could it be that we have become focused on our own needs to the exclusion (or at least the minimization) of the needs of the lost? Perhaps we are still zealous for mission in the sense of foreign mission. That is as it should be. However, *America is an enormous mission field. The United States is home to the third largest number of non-Christian people in the world. Only China and India have larger populations of non-Christian people than America. The local church must become missional in its local perspective.*

Helping Believers Cross Social and Cultural Boundaries

The homogeneous unit principle, first suggested by Donald McGavran in his 1955 *The Bridges of God*, states simply that people prefer to become Christians without crossing cultural or social boundaries, including socioeconomic and sociopolitical, boundaries. McGavran has received a lot of criticism over the years because he suggested that it was initially acceptable to work with people on this basis. People could be evangelized and converted within the framework of their own cultural or social group so that initially they were not required to cross boundaries that made them uncomfortable—in some cases so uncomfortable that the conversion process would be disrupted if they were forced to cross barriers they were not ready to cross.

McGavran's point was never that new believers of a specific cultural or social group or class be allowed to remain a separate, isolated group. His point was that winning people to Christ and teaching them to be what God wants them to be (and allowing time for growth, change and maturity) are two separate processes and must be understood as such. People can become believers within the context of their own cultural or social class or group. But they cannot remain culturally or socially isolated. They must grow in their faith and likeness of God to the point where they not only can but want to cross cultural, social, and class boundaries, interacting with people who are culturally or socially *other* (different) but loved by God and in need of his grace and mercy.

While many people disagree with McGavran, I believe he was right. He understood the basic human inclination toward likeness or sameness. People like to be with people who are like them. This inclination is not sinful. However, it can become sinful if it is allowed to grow into dislike or animosity toward people who are of a different group. Whether or not we agree with McGavran's observations about using the homogeneous unit principle in mission and outreach, we must admit that one of the challenges facing the Lord's church today is the need for believers to actively and effectively cross the cultural and social boundaries that dissect not only our Western society, but virtually all contemporary urban metropolises.

Jehu Hanciles has written about the missiological implications of global migration trends for the twenty-first century church (2003:146-156). His point in that article is that Christianity, as a religion of migration, has been spread through the various migration patterns of the past, and that the current global migrations continue to have a positive impact on mission. However, not all people who migrate are believers, and the astonishing statistics to which Hanciles refers represent both a significant challenge and opportunity for outreach both globally and locally.

According to the 2000 U.S. Census, in the decade between 1990 and 2000, there was an increase of 32.7 million people in U.S. population. For the first time in the 20th century, every State in the Union gained in population, with the greatest growth occurring in the West and South (2002:261). The fastest growing States were all in the West: Nevada, Arizona, Colorado, Utah and Idaho. More than 80% of all U.S. residents (over 226 million) live in metropolitan areas. While 75.1 percent of the American population is White, 12.3 is Black, and 12.5 is Latino. Latinos now make up the largest minority population in the U.S. People of other language groups are also present in significant numbers. For instance, there are over 70 language groups represented among the children enrolled in the Dallas Independent School District, in Dallas, Texas, a relatively small school district when compared, for example, to Los Angeles or New York (DISD 2003).

What are the implications of these migration realities? On a global scale, current migration trends mean that many missionaries in foreign urban contexts will encounter people from cultures other than the local indigenous culture who have migrated to that place in search of something not available to them in their home culture (security, freedom, economic opportunities, etc.). If sufficient numbers of a specific people group are present, there will be opportunities to establish a church within that people group. If sufficient numbers of that people are not present to establish a church for that people group, those people can be incorporated into existing local churches. Such multiethnic incorporation presents challenges, but with each challenge comes an opportunity.

The missiological implications of current global migration trends are much the same for Western local churches. The people of the world have come to America. Believers in American churches, already divided (to a degree) along economic and ethnic boundaries, must be confronted with the need to think differently about associations with people of other ethnic groups.

It is difficult for a church to become a multiethnic church. One of the first steps in the process of outreach to people of different ethnic groups is for believers to be willing to cross cultural boundaries, reaching out to people who are not yet part of the community of believers. Given the conflict between Jews and Gentiles in the first century, the New Testament provides plenty of sermon material related to ethnic and cross-cultural challenges the church faces today. Church leaders need to spend less time talking about issues and problems related to the felt needs of members (which reflects an internal focus) and redirect the church's attention to the needs of people who do not yet know God. The church must have an outward focus—one that looks across the social and ethnic boundaries that divide us so that we see the needs of people who are *other*.

This will not happen automatically. Learning to focus attention on the needs of people who are different than we are requires specific and intentional teaching designed to bring about that specific result. This was McGavran's point when he first suggested thinking about the Great Commission as a two-step process: 1) go make disciples, and 2) teach them to obey all things Jesus commanded. People may come to the Lord within the confines of their own sociocultural and socioeconomic group (their homogeneous group). But then they must be taught to look beyond that group to see the value of all people, to identify their needs, and reach out to them in love and devotion. Some of them will not respond because they prefer not to cross cultural boundaries and engage a group of people who have ethnic backgrounds different from their own. However, many people will respond to cross-cultural outreach and eagerly embrace the Good News, becoming part of the local church. Local church leaders must be ready to meet the worship and fellowship needs of the new believers. That is where an awareness of the various models for becoming a cross-cultural church become helpful.

One of Luke's goals in preparing his two-volume treatise was to confront his Jewish readers with the need to think beyond the confines of their own cultural group. They needed to learn to cross social and cultural boundaries in an effort to reach out to those who did not already enjoy a relationship with God. They would have been happy to perpetuate their homogeneous perspective. God, however, was not happy with that prospect. He required a broadening of their view. He requires that same broadening today.

Developing Avenues for Holistic Outreach and Ministry to the Marginalized in Local Communities

Luke mentions more categories of marginalized people more often than any other New Testament writer. Obviously he was interested in their status. His point was to demonstrate how Jesus and his original followers were interested in and ministered to marginalized people. Clearly, as far as Luke was concerned, ministry to marginalized people is essential if believers are to be obedient to the Great Commandment and the Great Commission. But what kind of ministry to marginalized people? For Luke, outreach to marginalized people was holistic in nature. It included not only proclamation, but also demonstration.

How can believers in local churches be involved in holistic outreach? Without a structure within the local church designed to assist members in holistic outreach it is difficult. Church leaders must take the initiative and establish programs or linkages to existing programs outside the local church so believers can engage in holistic outreach and ministry through established channels.

While it is certainly possible for believers to go out among the marginalized of society on their own, not many will have the experience or means to carry on an effective ministry without the benefit of an established structure. Suburban churches can establish working relationships with inner city churches or parachurch agencies where believers can do volunteer work. But many local churches can also, with a little creative thinking and funding, establish their own programs of holistic outreach. For instance, churches that have an involvement minister could redefine that position to *minister of holistic outreach*. That individual's job could be to prepare believers (through teaching and training) for "involvement" in holistic outreach. He or she can design programs and establish relationships with other churches and parachurch agencies, providing believers with avenues of outreach. If the person to be designated as minister of holistic outreach is not presently qualified for such a position, the church can provide educational opportunities that will broaden his or her capabilities. A number of schools and seminaries, especially those that specialize in missiological training, offer courses in urban/inner city ministry.

The point is that local church leaders must make holistic outreach and ministry a priority in their church. They must teach, train, and motivate believers regarding holistic outreach and ministry, and must provide them with avenues of service.

Making Room For The Holy Spirit In Non-Charismatic Churches

The issue between charismatic and non-charismatic believers is not so much what the Spirit did in the past, but what he may or may not be doing today, that is, whether or not the Spirit continues to give believers charismatic gifts today. The modern charismatic movement traces its roots to the Azusa Street Mission in Los Angeles, California in the early 1900s (McGrath 1997: 125). The movement gained greater acceptance in the 1960s and is currently the fastest growing segment of the Christian community (Barrett and Johnson 2003: 27.1 24-25).

Proponents of Pentecostalism have argued that Christian literature as early has second century (for instance, Justin Martyr in his *Dialogue with Trypho*), and throughout Christian writings thereafter, contain references to spiritual gifts, thereby providing evidence that God's Spirit has always been active when and where people were open to his work (Gromacki 1967:12). Those not inclined toward the Pentecostal view have pointed out that the references to spiritual gifts in historical Christian writings tend to be rather vague. For instance, in his *Dialogue with Trypho*, Justin Martyr refers to the presence of "spiritual gifts," but he does not elaborate on them. How do we know he is referring to the charismatic gifts of unlearned languages, healings, prophecy and the like?

My point in this section is not to address the ongoing (and likely unending) debate between charismatic and non-charismatic believers regarding the exact nature of the present work of the Holy Spirit. I am not charismatic and do not believe that the Holy Spirit continues to provide believers with the same kinds of spiritual gifts we see exhibited by believers in the first century. However, to say that the Holy Spirit is not carrying on the same charismatic gift ministry he did in the first century, is not to say that he is doing nothing!

For non-charismatic believers the question is, if the Holy Spirit is not engaged in the same gifting ministry in which he was engaged in the first century, but neither is he merely floating around doing nothing, what is he doing? He's doing a great deal and would like to do even more.

The Holy Spirit is given to believers as a gift. Surely, as that part of God who lives in each of us he is active. He would be even more active if believers would let him. He would like to make a difference in our lives. When Paul wrote to the believers in Rome and in the region of Galatia, he spoke of believers *following* the Spirit and *giving control* of their lives to the Spirit, who would lead them and change them, producing spiritual results in their lives (Rom.8:5-14; Gal. 5:16-25) (Dunn 1975:312). John spoke of the Spirit teaching believers (1 Jn. 2:20-27). The Spirit prays for us, intercedes for us, and empowers us to be the people God wants us to be (Rom. 8:26-27; Eph. 3:16).

The Spirit is given to us to make a difference in our lives. But for many non-charismatic believers, the Holy Spirit has little opportunity to make much of a difference because we have not been taught what he will do for us if we ask him to. We have not been taught that we must give him the authority he needs in our lives to make the needed changes. The Holy Spirit will not simply take up residence in our hearts on the day of our baptism and begin making changes in our lives. He must be invited to work; he must be given the authority to make the necessary adjustments.

For the most part, non-charismatic believers know all of this—at least on an intellectual level. But we don't seem to do anything with it. Few of us (though perhaps more today than a few years ago) invite the Holy Spirit to take control of our lives and lead us into a greater understanding of the Scriptures, or to change us, making us better people so we can reflect God's image more clearly. Why is this? Probably because naturalistic people, as most Western believers are, are uncomfortable with supernaturalistic things. It is a shame that our Western rationalistic, naturalistic worldview keeps us from enjoying one of the greatest blessings and sources of spiritual strength that God has given us.

Believers in non-charismatic churches need teaching that will lead them to acknowledge and depend on the Holy Spirit for insight, wisdom, inner strength and spiritual change and maturity. They need to expect him to lead and guide, as he did in the early church—especially in outreach and mission. How can this be accomplished? Leaders must teach and model that which they want believers to embrace and internalize. We need leaders whose lives evidence the presence of the Spirit, leaders who follow the Spirit, giving him control of their lives, allowing him to continue to grow in the likeness of God. We need church leaders who model a Spirit-led life and then who teach believers how to enjoy a Spirit-led life.

The church today needs to make room for the Holy Spirit in its worship assemblies, in its Bible classes, in its business meetings and planning sessions, and in the private devotions of both shepherds and sheep. The Spirit may not be doing exactly the same things he did in the first century church. But neither is he simply floating around doing nothing. He will be an active power and influence in a church if he is invited. He will guide and direct spiritual growth as well as outreach and mission just as he did in the first century—if we will allow him to do so.

Summary

Without a doubt, one could probably discover may more missiological implications in Luke's work. But these five provide us with enough to think about and act on for now. Local churches must:

1) develop a universal perspective,
2) understand that the church is missional in nature,
3) be willing to cross cultural and social boundaries to accomplish mission and ministry,
4) develop avenues for holistic outreach,
5) make room for the Holy Spirit to work in them.

Making progress in these five areas would allow local churches to be used more effectively by God as he accomplishes his mission in the world—the reconciliation of his estranged children.

WORKS CITED

Ash, Anthony Lee
1972 *The Gospel According To Luke Part 1 1:1-9:50.* Austin: Sweet.

Bamberger, B.J.
1962 "Tax Collector," in *The Interpreter's Dictionary of the Bible.* George Buttrick, ed. Nashville: Abingdon.

Barrett David B. and Todd M. Johnson
"Annual Statistical Table on Global Mission:2003," in *International Bulletin of Missionary Research.* Jonathan J. Bonk, ed.

Beasley-Murray, G. R.
1962 *Baptism in the New Testament.* Grand Rapids: Eerdmans.

Bell, Albert A.
1998 *Exploring the New Testament World: An Illustrated Guide to the World of Jesus and the First Christians.* Nashville: Nelson.

Blendinger, Christian
1975 "Disciple, Follow, Imitate, After," in *The New International Dictionary of New Testament Theology.* Colin Brown, ed. Grand Rapids: Zondervan.

Bock, Darrell L.
1994 Luke (1:1-9:50). *Baker Exegetical Commentary on the New Testament.* Grand Rapids: Baker.

Bruce, F. F.
    1954 *Commentary on the Book of Acts.* Grand
    Rapids: Eerdmans.

Conzelmann, Hans
    1961 *The Theology of St. Luke.* Philadelphia:
    Fortress.

Culpepper, R. Alan
    1995 "The Gospel of Luke," in *The New
    Interpreter's Bible.* Nashville: Abingdon.

Dallas Independent School District
    2002 *Inside DISD*
    www.dallasids.org/inside_disd/index.htm

Dollar, Harold E.
    1990 *A Biblical-Missiological Exploration of the
    Cross-cultural Dimensions in Luke-Acts.* Ph.D.
    dissertation, Fuller Theological Seminary.

Douglas, Mary
    1966 *Purity and Danger: An Analysis of Concepts
    of Pollution and Taboo.* London: Routledge and
    Kegan Paul.

Dunn, James D. G.
    1975 *Jesus and the Spirit: A Study of the Religious
    and Charismatic Experience of Jesus and the First
    Christians as Reflected in the New Testament.* Grand
    Rapids: Eerdmans.

Edersheim, Alfred
    1994 *Sketches of Jewish Social Life: Updated
    Edition.* Peabody: Hendrickson.

Elser, Philip Francis
   1987   *Community and Gospel in Luke-Acts: The
   Social and Political Motivations of Lucan Theology.*
   New York: Cambridge.

Ferguson, Everett
   1971   *Early Christians Speak.* Austin: Sweet.

Fitzmyer, Joseph A.
   1970   *The Gospel According to Luke I-IX.* New
   York: Doubleday.

   1998   *The Acts of the Apostles.* New York:
   Doubleday.

Geldenhuys, Norval
   1951   *Commentary of the Gospel of Luke.* Grand
   Rapids: Eerdmans.

Gilliland, Dean
   2000   "Contextualization," in *Evangelical
   Dictionary of World Missions.* A. Scott Moreau, ed.
   Grand Rapids: Baker.

Green Joel B.
   1997   *The Gospel of Luke.* Grand Rapids:
   Eerdmans.

Gromacki Robert G.
   1967   *The Modern Tongues Movement.*
   Philadelphia: Presbyterian and Reformed.

Guder, Darrell L.
   1998   *Missional Church: A Vision for the Sending of
   the Church in North America.* Grand Rapids:
   Eerdmans.

Hanciles, Jehu J.
2003 "Migration and Mission: Some Implications for the Twenty-first-Century Church," in *International Bulletin of Missionary Research*. Vol. 27, No. 4.

Harms, Richard B.
1999 *Missionary Paradigms From Luke-Acts For Multicultural Churches in the Twenty First Century*. D.Min. dissertation, Fuller Theological Seminary.

Heil, John Paul
1999 *The Meal Scenes in Luke-Acts: An Audience-Oriented Approach*. Atlanta: Society of Biblical Literature.

Hesselgrave, David J.
1997 Holistic Christianity? Yes! Holistic Mission? No!. . . and Yes! *Occasional Bulletin EMS* Spring 1997.

2003 The Poor: A Case of Mistaken Identity. *Evangelical Missions Quarterly*, 39 (2) 152-162.

Hiebert, Paul G.
1999 *Missiological Implications of Epistemological Shifts: Affirming Truth in a Modern/Postmodern World*. Harrisburg: Trinity.

Hiebert, Paul G., R. Daniel Shaw, and Tite Tiénou
1999 *Understanding Folk Religion: A Christian Response to Popular Beliefs and Practices*. Grand Rapids: Baker.

Hunsberger, George R. and Craig Van Gelder
1996 *The Church Between Gospel and Culture: The Emerging Mission in North America.* Grand Rapids: Eerdmans.

Hur Ju
2001 *A Dynamic Reading of the Holy Spirit in Luke-Acts.* Sheffield: Sheffield Academic Press.

Johnson, Timothy Luke
1992 "Luke-Acts, Book of," in *The Anchor Bible Dictionary.* David Noel Freedman, ed. New York: Doubleday.

Kearney, Michael
1986 *Worldview.* Novato: Chandler and Sharp.

Kidner, Derek F.
1994 "Isaiah," in *New Bible Commentary: 21st Century Edition.* D.A. Carson, et. al. eds. Downers Grove: InterVarsity.

Kosmin, Barry A and Egon Mayer
2001 *American Religious Identification Survey.* New York: The Graduate Center, City University of New York. http://www.gc.cuny.edu/studies/aris_index.htm 4/30/2003

Kraft, Charles H.
1979 *Christianity in Culture: A Study in Dynamic Biblical Theologizing in Cross-cultural Perspective.* MaryKnoll: Orbis.

2002 *Worldview For Christian Witness.* Prepublication edition. Pasadena: Fuller Theological Seminary.

Larkin, William J.
    1995 *Acts*. Downers Grove: InterVarsity.

    1998 "Mission in Luke," in *Mission in the New
    Testament: An Evangelical Approach*.
    William J. Larkin and Joel F. Williams, eds.
    Maryknoll: Orbis.

Liefeld, Walter L.
    1984 "Luke," in *The Expositor's Bible
    Commentary*. Frank Gæbelein, ed. Grand Rapids:
    Zondervan.

Longnecker, Richard N.
    1981 "The Acts of the Apostles," in *The Expositor's
    Bible Commentary*. Frank Gæbelein, ed. Grand
    Rapids: Zondervan.

Marshall, I. Howard
    1978 *The Gospel of Luke: A Commentary on the
    Greek Text*. Grand Rapids:Eerdmans.

Martin, Ralph P.
    1964 *Worship in the Early Church*. Grand Rapids:
    Eerdmans.

    1975 *New Testament Foundations: A Guide for
    Christian Students*. Grand Rapids:
    Eerdmans.

Maynard-Reid, Pedrito U.
    1997 *Complete Evangelism: The Luke-Acts Model*.
    Waterloo: Herald Press.

McConnell, Douglas
    2000 "Holistic Mission," in *Evangelical Dictionary
    of World Missions*. Grand Rapids: Baker.

McGavran, Donald
   1955   *The Bridges of God.* New York: Friendship
   Press.

McGrath, Alister E.
   1997   *Christian Theology: An Introduction.* Malden:
   Blackwell.

McKnight, Scot
   2000   "Proselytism and Godfearers," in *Dictionary
   of New Testament Background.* Craig Evans and
   Stanley Porter, eds. Downers Grove: InterVarsity.

Morris Linus J.
   1993   *The High Impact Church: A Fresh Approach
   to Reaching the Unchurched.* Thousand Oaks:
   Christian Associates International.

Müller, Dietrich
   1975   "Disciple, Follow, Imitate, After," in *The New
   International Dictionary of New Testament Theology.*
   Colin Brown, ed. Grand Rapids: Zondervan.

Murray, Stuart
   2001   *Church Planting: Laying Foundations.*
   Scottdale: Herald.

Myers, Bryant L.
   1999   *Walking with the Poor: Principles and
   Practices of Transformational Development.*
   Maryknoll: Orbis.

Neely, Alan
   2000   "Missiology," in *Evangelical Dictionary of
   World Missions.* A. Scott Moreau, ed. Grand Rapids:
   Baker.

Netland, Harold
2001 *Encountering Religious Pluralism: The Challenge to Christian Faith and Mission.* Downers Grove: InterVarsity.

Newbigin, Leslie
1986 *Foolishness to the Greeks: The Gospel and Western Culture.* Grand Rapids: Eerdmans.

Newman, Barclay and Eugene Nida
1972 *A Translator's Handbook on the Acts of the Apostles.* New York: United Bible Society.

Neyrey, Jerome H.
1991 "Ceremonies in Luke-Acts: The Case of Meals and Table-Fellowship," in *The Social World of Luke-Acts: Models for Interpretation.* Jerome Neyrey, ed. Peabody: Hendrickson.

Nissen, Johannes
1999 *New Testament and Mission: Historical and Hermeneutical Perspectives.* Frankfurt: Peter Lang.

Oakman, Dougles E.
1991 "The Countryside in Luke-Acts," in *The Social World of Luke-Acts: Models for Interpretation.* Jerome H. Neyrey, ed. Peabody: Hendrickson.

Peters, George W.
1972 *A Biblical Theology of Missions.* Chicago: Moody.

Pilgrim, Walter E.
1982 *Good News to the Poor: Wealth and Poverty in Luke-Acts.* Minneapolis: Augsburg.

Roth, S. John
1997 *The Blind, the Lame, and the Poor: Character Types in Luke-Acts*. Sheffield: Sheffield Academic Press.

Seccombe, David Peter
1982 *Possessions and the Poor in Luke-Acts*. Linz: SNTU.

Seitz, Christopher R.
2001 Isaiah 40-66. *The New Interpreter's Bible*. Leander Keck, ed. Nashville: Abingdon.

Shelton, James B.
1991 *Mighty in Word and Deed: The Role of the Holy Spirit in Luke-Acts*. Peabody: Hendrickson.

Staples, W. E.
1962 "Chronology of the N.T.," in *Interpreters Dictionary of the Bible*. George Buttrick, ed. Nashville: Abingdon.

Stein, Robert H.
1992 "Luke." *The New American Commentary*. Nashville: Broadman.

Summers, Ray
1972 *Commentary on Luke*. Waco: Word.

Sweetland, Dennis M.
1990 *Our Journey with Jesus: Discipleship According to Luke-Acts*. Collegeville: Liturgical Press.

Toombs, L. E.
1962 "Clean and Unclean," in *Interpreters Dictionary of the Bible*. George Buttrick, ed. New York: Abingdon.

Van Engen, Charles
1991 *God's Missionary People: Rethinking the Purpose of the Local Church*. Grand Rapids: Baker.

1996 *Mission on the Way: Issues in Mission Theology*. Grand Rapids: Baker.

Van Rheenen, Gailyn and Bob Waldron
2002 *The Status of Missions: A Nationwide Survey of Churches of Christ*. Abilene: ACU Press.

Wall, Robert W.
2002 "The Acts of the Apostles," in *The New Interpreter's Bible*. Leander Keck, ed. Nashville: Abingdon.

Wan, Enoch
2000 "Ethnocentrism," in *Evangelical Dictionary of World Mission*. A. Scott Moreau, ed. Grand Rapids: Baker.

Watts, John D.
1987 *Isaiah 34-66: Word Biblical Commentary*. David Hubbard and Glenn Barker, eds. Waco: Word.

Weder, Hans
1992 "Disciple, Discipleship," in *Anchor Bible Dictionary*. David Freedman, Ed. New York: Doubleday.

Wilkins, Michael
1992 "Discipleship," in *Dictionary of Jesus and the Gospels*. Joel Green, Scot McKnight, and I. Howard Marshall, eds. Downers Grove: InterVarsity Press.

Willimon, William H.
1988 *Acts: Interpretation, A Bible Commentary for Teaching and Preaching*. Atlanta: John Knox.

Winter, Ralph D. and Bruce A Koch
1999 "Finishing the Task: The Unreached Peoples Challenge," in *Perspectives on the World Christian Movement*. Ralph Winter and Steven Hawthorne, eds. Pasadena, William Carey.

Wright, David P.
1992 "Unclean and Clean," in *Anchor Bible Dictionary*. David Noel Freedman, ed. New York: Doubleday.

Wright, John W.
2002 *The New York Times 2002 Almanac*. New York: Penguin. John Wright, ed.

CPSIA information can be obtained at www.ICGtesting.com
Printed in the USA
LVOW13s0936051013

355580LV00002B/470/A